Praise for *The Last Prairie*, by Stephen R. Jones

"[A] gem of Great Plains environmental writing. Stephen Jones has given us a collection of his undated journal entries that represent an interesting combination of nature writing, history, and anecdote. . . . One finds the footprints of Mari Sandoz, Aldo Leopold, and John Neihardt in this must-read for Sandhills enthusiasts. As Jones's own 'love song to the plains,' *The Last Prairie* captures the region's rich history with a depth often overlooked in other writings on the Great Plains."
—DOUGLAS HARVEY, *Journal of the West*

"Reading this book is as pleasant an experience as actually viewing the tall, gently waving prairie grasses and pastoral scenes that Jones describes."
—*Library Journal*

"Jones does a remarkable job of capturing the variety, texture, and integrity of the Sandhills environment—including the plant and animal life as well as the ranching community and the historical fabric that work to create this complicated landscape. . . . [*The Last Prairie*] richly describes a region of the United States that few people might be familiar with. Second, it works to show how landscape, wildlife, culture, and history are always interconnected. . . . Finally, the book works to make a compelling argument that because of human dependence upon and connection to landscape and all life, regions like the Sandhills deserve consideration and preservation."
—SARAH HULME HILL, *Western American Literature*

"A must-read book."
—JONIS AGEE, author of *Strange Angels*

"A lovely book, to enjoy and cherish."
—ANN H. ZWINGER, author of *The Nearsighted Naturalist* and *Beyond the Aspen Grove*

T0312501

"From insect to eagle's-eye view, *The Last Prairie* gives us the heartening illuminations of a writer honoring his chosen cut of the continent with loyal affection and full, gifted attention."

—MERRILL GILFILLAN, author of *Magpie Rising* and *Chokecherry Places*

....

"This book is a celebration of place by a man who truly loves it, walks it, and is willing to work hard enough to bring it home to readers and place it in our hearts."

—CHRISTINA NEALSON, author of *Living on the Spine: A Woman's Life in the Sangre de Cristo Mountains*

....

Stephen R. Jones

Nourishing Waters, Comforting Sky

Thirty-Five Years at a Sandhills Oasis

University of Nebraska Press
Lincoln

Portions of this book previously appeared, in different form, in R. A. Adams, ed., *Into the Night* (Boulder: University Press of Colorado, 2013); and "Trumpeter Swans Return," *Nebraska Life*, July/August 2018.

The University of Nebraska Press is part of a land-grant institution with campuses and programs on the past, present, and future homelands of the Pawnee, Ponca, Otoe-Missouria, Omaha, Dakota, Lakota, Kaw, Cheyenne, and Arapaho Peoples, as well as those of the relocated Ho-Chunk, Sac and Fox, and Iowa Peoples.

Publication of this volume was assisted by a grant from the Friends of the University of Nebraska Press.

Library of Congress Cataloging-in-Publication Data
Names: Jones, Stephen R., 1947– author.
Title: Nourishing waters, comforting sky: thirty-five years at a sandhills oasis / Stephen R. Jones.
Description: Lincoln: University of Nebraska Press, [2022] | Includes bibliographical references.
Identifiers: LCCN 2021035832
ISBN 9781496230270 (paperback)
ISBN 9781496231574 (epub)
ISBN 9781496231581 (pdf)
Subjects: LCSH: Sand dune ecology—Nebraska—Sandhills. | Sand dune conservation—Nebraska—Sandhills. | Sandhills (Neb.) | Crescent Lake National Wildlife Refuge (Neb.) | BISAC: NATURE / Ecosystems & Habitats / Plains & Prairies | NATURE / Regional
Classification: LCC QH105.N2 J67 2022 | DDC 577.5/83097827—dc23/eng/20211007
LC record available at https://lccn.loc.gov/2021035832

Set in Questa by Mikala R. Kolander.

For my mother, Kay Kelly Jones

Contents

Author's Note

The place I refer to as Pine Lake appears under a different name on modern maps, but for all other places mentioned in the book, including Crescent Lake, Lakeside, and Pine Creek, I've used the widely accepted European American names.

In places, I have described or quoted from printed transcriptions of Plains Indian origin and hero stories. My purpose in doing this is to provide understanding of the intimate and loving relationship that indigenous peoples of the western plains have maintained with the prairie and all its inhabitants, and not to characterize or interpret religious belief.

There is a growing movement, supported by prominent naturalists and members of the American Ornithological Society, toward eliminating patronymic names of birds and other animals. In this book I've substituted "woodland hawk" for "Cooper's hawk," and "juniper solitaire" for "Townsend's solitaire."

While we chose not to include photos in this book, screen-size images of most of the plants, animals, and places described can be found on my professional website: https://www.sandhillsolitude .org/.

Royalties from this book will be donated equally to Native American charities that support indigenous land recovery and to nonprofits that support Sandhills wildlife refuges.

Nourishing Waters, Comforting Sky

Portal in the Sky

A story shared by the Cheyenne, Lakota, and other Plains Indian cultures tells of a time when two teenage sisters sat on a hilltop admiring the stars. The evening breeze had retreated to its hiding place behind the mountains, and no sounds came from the camp down in the hollow. Nothing seemed to stir, not even the meadow voles curled up in their grass nests or the little mole crickets listening from the mouths of their burrows.

The older girl spoke in a whisper, reluctant to wake the stillness, "That star up there to the right is very beautiful. I like that one."

"I like that other one better, the red one just above the horizon," answered her sister.

"Look at that one high overhead. See how brightly it shines, how silver is its light. I could marry that star."

The younger girl smiled. "If you marry that star, Older Sister, I'm afraid I will miss you very much."

The two sisters joined hands and walked back down the hillside toward their lodge, their deerskin dresses swishing through the waist-high grass.

The next morning they went walking among the ponderosa pines that clung to a rocky escarpment above camp. The older girl saw a porcupine snuffling its way through the pine duff. The porcupine's ebony and golden quills glowed in the autumn sunlight, and the girl wanted them for her deerskin dress. She tied some buffalo sinew to a pine branch to make a noose, grasped the branch in her right fist, and crept forward.

When the porcupine saw her coming, it waddled over to the nearest ponderosa. It had scrambled quite a way up, digging its sharp claws into the soft bark and anchoring its chubby body against the trunk with its stout tail, before the girl reached the base of the tree. She looped the noose around her neck and began climbing from branch to branch.

The porcupine ascended ever higher, and as it did, the tree seemed to grow taller.

"Come back," cried the younger sister. "You will climb all the way into the sky!"

The girl reached out and flung the noose toward the porcupine's head. But the sinew slid harmlessly off the animal's slippery fur and quills, and the porcupine wriggled free. She flung the noose three more times, and each time the porcupine slipped away. She heard her sister's voice far below.

"Come back, come back. This tree is bewitched. Please come back, or I will never see you again!"

The air grew frigid and damp. When the girl looked down, she could see only white. Above her, the porcupine had transformed into a ghostlike shape that seemed to float in the swirling clouds. She began to feel dizzy, and she wrapped her arms around the trunk as the wind whipped the crown back and forth. She closed her eyes and held on tight, her arms and legs shaking with fear.

Just when she felt like she could hold on no longer, the tree stopped swaying, and she felt the warmth of the sun on her cheeks. She opened her eyes to a world of green hills and soft ocher light. She stepped off the tree branch and began walking toward the sun.

Before long she saw a figure standing on top of a low hill. She knelt on the ground, lowered her head, and waited. She knelt there for a long time, trembling and too afraid to move. When she finally summoned the courage to look up, she saw a tall man with flowing silver hair standing over her.

"Come with me now," he said.

The girl began to shake convulsively, and tears streamed down her cheeks.

"What's the matter with you? Just last night you said you wanted to marry me."

"Are you . . . ?"

"Yes, I'm the star you were talking to last night."

He held out his hand and she took it and followed him over the hills.

He married her and built her a fine lodge and brought her fresh game and gifts from the prairie. They slept together on a soft buffalo robe, and every morning she built a fire and prepared him a rich meat stew to sustain him during his morning hunt.

While he was away she would go out with the other women to gather wild plants. They dug up many kinds of root plants, but there was one special kind, called *timpsula*, with fuzzy stems and green leaves in the shape of a human hand, that she was not to dig up.

"To dig up that plant is bad medicine, and it is forbidden," her husband told her.

"Why is it forbidden?"

"I cannot tell you, but it is very bad medicine."

She couldn't stop thinking about the forbidden plant. At night she dreamed of its silvery stems, shimmering in the moonlight, and in the morning when she awoke, the taste of its earthy, succulent root lingered on her tongue.

One morning the young woman stood looking at one of these forbidden plants, wondering how it could possibly be against the medicine to harvest them. After pondering for a long time, she decided to go ahead and dig it up.

"I'll just take a bit, and see what happens," she thought.

It took her most of the morning to scrape her way down to the bottom of the giant root. When she finally pulled the root free, she saw that it made a hole in the ground. She peered down through the hole and gasped. Clear as sunlight, but far, far below, lay the village of her people.

She saw the lodges, sparkling white with whisps of gray smoke curling up from their peaks. She saw laughing children and pinto horses playing in the clear waters of the meandering stream. She saw bison snorting and stomping in the greening meadows. She heard the cooing of mourning doves, the clicking sounds of the little grasshoppers, the rush of the wind through the bending willows, the murmur of human voices. She saw her younger sister, sad and serenely beautiful, standing beside the lodge entrance and gazing up toward the clouds.

As the young woman watched, her sister picked up a gourd and walked down to the stream to get water. When she reached the stream, she heard rumbling overhead. She knelt down and gently lowered the gourd into the water, being careful not to disturb the glassy surface. When she rose and turned back toward camp, she felt the first raindrops strike her forehead and cheeks.

Lightning crackled right above her, and the swirling vortex of cloud let loose a torrent. She paused and glanced back toward camp, then set the gourd down onto the grassy stream bank and stood facing the storm. She threw her head back and opened her arms to the sky, feeling the wind whip through her hair while the cool liquid trickled down her face and flowed over her breast.

"Sister, oh sister, why have you forsaken me?"

Her high keening voice cut through the rushing rain and floated up into the heavens as she closed her eyes and savored the bittersweet taste of her sister's tears.

The story continues with various twists and turns, but it's that one alluring image of a perfect but unreachable village on the verdant prairie that has haunted my dreams. The young woman's pangs of separation and longing mirror the sadness that so many of us feel after first setting out on our own. The vision of her serene home, revealed through a porthole in the clouds, awakens us to all we've lost and destroyed.

We have become stranded in an alien world of freeways, strip malls, and yellow skies. For hundreds of thousands of years, our species lived in communion with the rippling grasses, sheltering forests, clear flowing streams, and thriving wildlife of this sacred Earth. Now we experience only glimpses of these treasures.

We grow homesick not just for our family and place of birth but also for the bond with nature that sustained and comforted our species until very recently. Every once in a while we experience sudden awakenings, times when we feel an exquisite connection with the world around us. Then the portal closes, and we return to our cluttered lives, wondering if it will ever open again.

For each of us there are singular moments, sudden accidents in life, that help to define our separate journey. While seventeen and living with my parents and two brothers in Northern California, I was trying to perform a dismount maneuver called a "bar snap" on a horizontal bar in the backyard. When I swung under the bar, kicked out, and pushed off, my right hand got stuck, and something snapped between my shoulder blades. After I hobbled into the house, the searing pain made me so dizzy I finally fainted and cracked my head on the side of the bathtub.

For reasons that no one truly understands, I kept reinjuring the muscle and the pain kept coming back. It became such a crippling part of me that by the time I was thirty, I had to reconstruct my life from scratch.

Now, living in Boulder, Colorado, I traded full-time teaching and graduate studies for teaching English and high school equivalency classes in the evening and studying wildlife populations during the daytime, often while lying flat on my back. I learned how to write without using pen or keyboard. I gave up strumming the guitar and got serious about photography. I learned to meditate, quieting my thoughts and emotions until I imagined my heartbeats synchronizing with the natural rhythms around me.

Extreme optimists say that our physical limitations—and we all have them—can be seen as gifts. They challenge us and help us find our true direction. My handicap steered me toward becoming a naturalist—a person who goes out alone to study and write about nature. It enabled me to experience intimate relationships with golden eagles and monarch butterflies. It gave me the patience to learn the songs of birds and the ways of beetles. I wouldn't trade my life for any other.

But living with an ill-defined handicap can become daunting. It's a challenge to program physical activities so that you do enough to keep moving forward but don't over exert and send things into a tailspin. The condition is invisible and not something most people understand.

Under these circumstances, a periodic break from daily responsibilities feels especially welcome. Forty years ago, without consciously thinking about it, I chose the North American prairie as my place of retreat and healing.

On the prairie I found both peace and a sense of expansive

opportunity. Part of the appeal came from the serenity, the glowing morning light and fiery sunsets, the abundant wildlife and limitless vistas. The biggest reward was a chance to interact with nature for days on end without the distraction of human voices or physical obligation.

After exploring the prairie region for several years, I finally made it to the Nebraska Sandhills, twenty thousand square miles of mostly native grassland and thriving wetlands populated by jackrabbits, curlews, trumpeter swans, sharp-tailed grouse, and a few thousand family ranchers who have stewarded the land for five generations. As I became attuned to the textures of this luxuriant and seemingly boundless prairie, I rediscovered a kinship with the earth that awakened feelings of warmth and belonging. I felt like I'd returned to a cherished, long-forgotten home.

Now I camp out alone in the Sandhills for several weeks each year, and I always return home invigorated and more optimistic about life. I would never expect those old pangs of separation and yearning to fade completely away. After all, they are part of the price of admission.

Their ebb and flow help keep us attuned to the myriad joys and sorrows that enrich our path. And on the best of days, those primal feelings, combined with some focused observation, have helped me to see the world in all its wonder, as if for the first time.

Timpsula

It had sprinkled off and on since sunset. The first crack of thunder jolted me awake around midnight, and I lay in the tent counting the time between the flashes and thunderclaps. One one thousand, two one thousand . . . So long as the interval remained five seconds or more, indicating one mile, I'd stay hunkered down rather than making a mad dash for the car, parked down along the lakeshore.

The sky flickered overhead and the whole tent lit up for a microsecond. Even after the darkness had smothered the light, my eyes retained a clear image of the blue nylon walls, my hiking boots piled carelessly at the foot of the blue-and-black sleeping bag, the dirty red pack resting on the floor to the left—a snapshot of peaceful home, here on the prairie. Then, "boom!" The earth shook and the aftershocks echoed off the clouds and cascaded over the hills.

I grabbed my flute and held it tight in both hands. A Caddo Indian friend had carved it from red cedar. He said that the red cedar was the home of the thunderbird and would protect me from lightning. He said that when I blew on the flute my breath would merge with the breath of all my ancestors, forming a perfect union. The wood smelled like incense and felt pliant. I played a few notes as lightning rent the sky and peels of thunder shook the earth.

The flashes eased off a little, just as the first large drops splattered on the rain fly. I opened the tent flap to better smell the rain and hear the night sounds. A few chorus frogs had started up in the marsh at the upper end of the lake, and their calm, rhythmic chirruping played counterpoint to the hiss of the rain in the pines and the low grumbling of the receding thundercloud.

Then the wind came whooshing across the dunes and the sky

let loose. I sat up in my sleeping bag drinking in the sound of the rushing rain. I thought again of my mother.

"I've never seen such rain," she would say while sitting in the living room of our Northern California home, framed by the water-color murals she'd created of swirling Koi carp and misty Asian mountains. She'd throw the patio doors open and let the spray and smell of wet grass and wisteria permeate the house.

"Isn't it marvelous?"

Kay grew up on a farm in the Salinas Valley, where furnace-like summer winds fill your clothes with grit and suck the saliva from the roof of your mouth. She'd ride her horse, Midnight, for hours over the parched hills and down through the sun-seared dunes along the dry riverbed, her silky auburn hair flowing out behind her. The two things she hated most were rattlesnakes and wind.

Rain was a gift. That's how it is in the arid West. You spend half your time staring up at the sky, hoping that single shaft of cool purple, extending down from the nearest popcorn cloud, will come your way. Save the crops. Keep enough grass growing so you won't have to sell half your stock. Keep the garden from becoming a grasshopper cafeteria.

The stray rain cloud rarely makes it to where you're standing; simple geometry practically precludes that, but you hope anyway. Then, when you're paying no attention to the weather, the rain and hail come blasting down out of a mostly blue sky. Here in the Sandhills it can be dead calm and ninety degrees one minute, tornadoes and flying catfish the next. So you savor every drop, not knowing when the next storm will come your way.

Every time a big storm swirled down from the Gulf of Alaska and slammed into the California coast, I would call Kay on the phone and ask her what it was like.

"Oh, hardly anything here. It's all up north. But my kites are back."

When the emphysema had charred her lungs to the point that she spent the whole day sitting on the couch, reaching down hard for every breath, she still had the birds, and the rain.

"I'm afraid the storms will drive the kites away."

When I was visiting her in California, Kay would worry that all the birds would be gone and there wouldn't be anything for me to watch while lounging in the backyard. She never fully understood that I simply liked being there with her. The birds were a way for each of us to pretend that the other felt better.

"Did you see the kites?" she would ask.

"Yes, and your Cooper's hawk, and a golden eagle, and dozens of yellow-rumped warblers. It's a veritable menagerie out there."

I helped her make a list, and she shared it with a friend or two.

And then two nights after she died, my wife, Nancy, and I were sleeping at the house and we heard something squawking and hooting on the patio outside the bedroom window. One bird was crying out like a youngster begging for food, the other barking out its territorial call: "Whut, whut-whut, wheew."

The next morning we added northern spotted owl to my mother's backyard bird list. It seemed right that the last entry was both a threatened species and a member of the owl clan, the ghost birds. The owls provided a measure of comfort and reminded me of what bonded my mother and me so close: our mutual passion for nature.

Every few days for almost a year I reached for the phone, wanting to talk to my mother—about the scary doings in Washington, Tiger Woods, Jane Austen, Highland adventures of veterinarian James Herriot, my discoveries on the prairie, the kites and owls in her backyard. I couldn't forget that when we arrived at the empty house the day after her death, we found two objects sitting on the table where she had been eating breakfast: her wedding band, left there by the fire rescue crew, and a Rand McNally Atlas in which she had circled all the places on the prairie where I had camped that spring.

I lived with that image and the emotions that went with it for a couple of years, until I realized that they weren't likely to fade away on their own. Finally, I forced myself back to this quiet lake in the heart of the Nebraska Sandhills, the place on earth I love most.

I'd camp by myself here for a few nights every other month, around the time of the full moon, and let the earth help with the healing. I decided to rededicate myself to discovering everything imaginable about this one place.

So I lay awake on this early June evening listening to the rain and thinking about my mother as one thunderstorm after another rumbled across the hills. When I finally went back to sleep, it was almost dawn. When I awoke again, little puddles of rainwater had formed inside the tent.

I heard my owls—the local great horned pair—hooting in the ponderosas on the hillside above the tent. Their mellifluous voices and my soggy feet were just enough to get me motivated. And also, the faint hope of finding the first, elusive prairie turnips blooming among sandstone outcrops north of the lake.

Since first reading about the prairie turnip, the sacred, wild tuber of the Arapahos, Cheyennes, Lakotas, Pawnees, and other western tribes, I had equated it with plants like ghost orchid and frankincense, mythical wonders I never expected to see in this lifetime. To find a prairie turnip growing here in the Sandhills would feel like discovering a gold nugget lying in the grass. And to taste one—to savor that same earthy succulence that nourished and sustained the peoples of the plains for generations—seemed beyond worthiness.

So important was the prairie turnip to the Lakotas after they migrated west from the Minnesota lake country that they called it *timpsula*, which translates roughly as "little wild rice of the prairie." The Osages called it simply *dogoe*, or "potato," and the Winnebago named it *tdokewihi*, meaning "hungry." The Blackfeet christened two buttes north of the Missouri after the prairie turnips that grew on their grassy slopes, and they used the plants ceremonially during their annual sun dance.

Plains Indian women would dig up the tough, goose-egg-sized tubers in midsummer. They located them in late spring when the flowers bloomed for a week or two. But if you dug them up then, you'd often find only a shriveled root where the starchy tuber should be. So the diggers marked the location and waited until later, just before the withered stalks broke off and scattered like tumbleweeds across the prairie. By then the ground had usually grown rock hard, so the women used a pointed digging stick that had been tempered by fire.

Sometimes children came along to help find the plants, after being instructed that the finger-like leaves of each prairie turnip point in the direction of others. Like participants in an Easter egg hunt, the children scattered across the grass, shouting out their discoveries.

After returning to camp, women would braid the roots together with sinew, smoke them, and hang them up for winter. Ethnobotanist Melvin Gilmore reported that four braided strings of prairie turnips could fetch one basket of shelled corn or one buffalo robe in trade between tribes.

Plains Indians also pounded the roots into a coarse flour, used to thicken soups. They boiled them whole with bison meat or mashed them with chokecherries and jerky to create an earthy form of pemmican. Or sometimes they simply speared the tubers with a stick and roasted them over an open fire.

Lewis and Clark reported that grizzly bears dug up prairie turnips when the ground remained relatively soft in early summer. Former Corps of Discovery member John Coulter subsisted on the roots during his harrowing, and stark-naked, two-hundred-mile flight from Blackfoot captivity in 1808.

And then there was the Native American story of the young woman who married a star, defied him by uprooting a giant prairie turnip, and created a porthole in the clouds that enabled her to see her village and her people with loving clarity. Since first discovering the story, I'd listened to it online or read various translations a dozen times.

So, with the earthy taste of *timpsula* on my tongue, I put on some dry socks and my wet boots and crawled into the misty dawn. The mile-wide lake had turned to gold as the rising sun filtered through the fog. Out in the middle, a half dozen white pelicans navigated languidly among rafts of western grebes and ruddy ducks. Black terns darted and dived over the still water.

The moist air smelled of fermenting pine needles and resonated with bird song. A curlew cried from the grass-covered dunes across the lake, and the staccato chatter of marsh wrens and guttural croaks of yellow-headed blackbirds burst out from the lakeside cattails. Orioles and goldfinches whistled in the cottonwoods and willows lining the near shore. A couple of coyotes yipped and squealed from the dunes to the west, beyond the pines, where the wet green grass glistened like frost in the morning sunlight.

Wrapped in the blanket of spring sounds, I wandered up through the strip of conifers that encircles the western and northern shorelines, looking for signs of terrestrial life. I found a dozen owl pellets scattered around the base of a mature pine and tracks of coyotes, cottontails, and white-tailed deer etched in the sandy soil. I followed the deer tracks through the woods, tunneling under the wet branches of several sprawling red cedars, until I came to a small clearing.

I rested in the meadow for a few minutes, waiting for the white-tailed doe. I always feel like an interloper up here, what with the dead calm, the sheltering pines, and the braided lines of heart-shaped tracks crisscrossing the sandy soil. This is the doe's place of refuge from the few anglers, campers, and hunters who frequent the lake. I usually sit here for a few minutes and try to let the doe find me before I stumble upon her.

One morning, while I lounged under a tree in the meadow, she sniffed her way to within arm's reach. As her ears and tail flicked nervously and her nostrils flared, I could sense her warm breath. Later I stumbled upon her turquoise-eyed fawn lying motionless in the grass fifty yards away.

Other mornings the doe stands on a little hill thirty yards from my tent and snorts. That little bit of disdain is infinitely preferable to the clatter of hoofs and the sight of her snow-white tail raised in alarm when I blunder into her territory and she bounds off in fright.

This morning, after waiting for several minutes, I finally saw her, not in the meadow but in the grass-covered dunes beyond the last pines. Her ruddy-red flanks, distended with fawn, glowed in the sunlight as she tiptoed calmly from one wild rosebush to another, meticulously nipping off the petals and withered fruits. She didn't seem to notice me, so I watched her until she topped a distant hill and disappeared on the far side. I got up, circled around to the right, and emerged from the woods a couple of hundred yards north of the meadow.

Here I joined the dirt track that parallels the marsh on the northwest side of the lake and followed it for a half mile to the outlet, a three-foot-wide stream of water flowing through a metal culvert. I worked my way down the right side of this little creek, which serpentined through a sedge-grass meadow where blond-naped bobolinks sang their tinkling arias from atop pale-green snowberry bushes.

To my left, six turkey vultures had lined up on six consecutive fence posts. One had stretched out its wings to soak up the sun. The other five appeared to be sleeping and paid little notice when I sidled toward them to snap a couple of photos. Overhead, a small flock of barn swallows circled and swooped in the blue.

A mile or two downstream, the stream meandered toward a modest outcrop where the sandy soil seemed more compacted and a variety of shorter grasses flourished. Prairie turnips aren't reputed to grow well in loose sand, so this outcrop seemed to offer my best hope.

A faint cattle trail traversed the slope above me and disappeared over the hilltop. I followed it and began to see wildflowers. Shell-leaf penstemons sprouted more than knee-high from the hillside on my right, their trumpet-shaped, pink blossoms still coated with dew. All around them silver cryptanthas, fuzzy members of the borage family with erect white flowers, glistened like minia-ture candelabras.

A shrill whistle revealed a rock wren perched atop a bare knoll. He bobbed up and down on spindly legs, flicking his long tail assert-ively. I searched all around for the culprit, and just when I was resigned to accepting the blame for the disturbance, saw a mangy, ill-fed coyote amble over the next ridge.

A little farther along I knelt down to examine a darkling bee-tle who had crawled up a dewy blade of fresh-sprouted grass. As I examined its long, beady antennae and narrow, black head, I noticed a lupine-like plant poking out of a patch of bare soil just to the left. My heart shifted into overdrive at the sight of the fuzzy stem, five-fingered leaves, and egg-shaped flower spike with lav-ender and white blossoms.

The plant was much smaller than I had expected, no more than eight inches high. It looked distinct from all other wild legumes I had ever seen, and I was certain it was the real thing, but for confirmation I extracted Jon Farrar's *Wildflowers of Nebraska and the Great Plains* from my pack. The legume matched the photograph in every respect, from the silvery hairs on the stems and finger-like leaves to the egg-shaped cluster of pea-like flowers.

As unassuming as the plant appeared, I still found my heart racing as I lay down beside it, inhaling the musty, peanut-like fragrance of its flowers and caressing the silky hairs lining the stem.

What to do next? Like the bison, prairie wolf, and elk, prairie turnips have been eliminated from much of their natural range, victims of cultivation and intensive grazing. And like the bison, prairie wolf, and elk, prairie turnips were once part of the sacred flow of life energy that bound millions of people to the prairie. The rituals and legends surrounding the harvesting and eating of this humble legume acknowledge not just the plant's importance as food but also its kinship to the earth, grass, and sky—all the material things that sustain us—and the Great Mystery that infuses everything with spirit and life.

But I really wanted to taste the root, not simply to say I'd tried it but to experience the sensory link between the *timpsula* and the cultures it has touched and nourished. Feeling eerily like wee Alice in the rabbit hole, I told myself, "I'll take just a small bite," and pulled out my pocket knife.

The soil offered little resistance, and I'd soon scraped out a shallow trench around the plant. I hesitated for a moment, not sure whether I should continue, then returned to scraping away, until the trench reached a couple of inches deep.

I heard a faint snapping sound and looked on in dismay as the stem and palm-like leaves listed to the right. I put the knife back in my pocket and hastily tamped the disturbed ground around the plant, trying to convince myself that the wound would heal.

My mother died alone while eating breakfast on a Monday morning, just thirty hours before Nancy and I were scheduled to arrive at the house. Her visiting healthcare aid found her sprawled out on the green linoleum floor among pieces of blood-red watermelon. The small white bowl with the serpentine gold pattern around the edge lay right-side-up beside her head. When the fire rescue team arrived, they took off her wedding band and placed it on the table. A police officer knocked on my door in Boulder an hour or so later.

"I have a message for you," he said. "You need to call this number."

I had never seen my mother more upset than the time, six months before, when she had scurried breathlessly to the side yard, where I was basking in the sun beside the Koi pond. Kay had excavated the pond with a shovel some years before, and after she'd hit bedrock, family and friends had worked together to line the pond with concrete.

"It's my wedding band," she said. "I must have washed it down the drain when I got out of the bathtub."

She appeared very upset but then reassured me.

"It's not really important. Just a wedding band."

I could see that it was very important, and I thought about my parents' sacred partnership, fifty years together, three children, all that suffering during the decade after my father died.

After a couple of days, we gave up looking. Then, Nancy was reading and lounging beside the pond one morning when she saw a glint of gold in the grass.

After Kay died, I carried her wedding band around in my wallet for a couple of years. When the wallet finally fell apart, I placed the band in a small rosewood box in my desk, so I could take it out from time to time and run it around the end of my ring finger.

I gazed back down at the *timpsula* and saw that it was still tilting limply to the right. I packed some more soil around it, then headed back for camp.

By now the air had grown hot, and I stopped in the woods to rest. There's a comfortable spot at the base of a rusty-barked ponderosa where it feels good to settle into the fragrant pine needles and watch the world go by. Crows and woodland hawks soar through this meadow, and a porcupine sometimes sleeps in the crown of an adjacent pine.

I waited for an hour but saw only a half dozen chipping sparrows and yellow-rumped warblers flitting through the canopy. The mid-morning breeze came sweeping in from the west, tossing the pine boughs. By the time I walked back down the hill toward camp, the pine needles beneath the trees had been sucked dry and the cicadas had struck up their weary chorus in the lakeside cottonwoods.

I extracted some white cheddar and a red pepper from the cooler and sat at a picnic table watching the willows bend and sway over the water as flocks of coots and grebes rode the foaming waves. An empty cattle truck rattled down the dirt road across the lake, skirted the bobolink meadow, and continued west toward a remote ranch. I could still see the dust swirling skyward and hear the engine's labored drone long after the truck had disappeared into the sun-bleached dunes.

Owls

I returned to Pine Lake for a few days in October. Early fall is a peaceful time in the Sandhills. Most days start off dead calm, with a dome of cobalt sky arching over amber hills. Frosty nights resonate with the hooting of owls and exuberant yips of coyotes. The Drying Grass Moon (Lakota name for the full moon closest to the autumn equinox) eases up above the eastern horizon around dusk for several consecutive nights, providing ample light for evening strolls through the woods and around the lake.

I set up my tent in my customary spot beneath the pines, where there's a clear view of the lake, the bordering cattail marshes, and across the water to the sea of rolling dunes. I'd chosen this spot many years before, during my first visit to the lake. Or more accurately, a pair of great horned owls had chosen it for me.

I'd been driving around the Sandhills for some time looking for a home base where I could camp out alone, photograph grasses and wildflowers, and study breeding bird populations, when I came upon this state wildlife area on a back road southwest of Gordon. At first glance the mile-wide lake seemed almost forlorn, with its murky, leach-infested water, rickety red picnic tables scattered across patches of mowed pasture grass, and aromatic outhouses buzzing with houseflies.

But the lake met my first requirement for prairie camping—solitude—and on this particular evening, no humans were around. Within minutes of setting up camp, I noticed the cottony sensation and faint humming in the ears that signals escape from perpetual background noise, the subliminal urban drone of modern life.

Just as the sun eased its way down behind the heaving hills to the west, two great horned owls flew in and landed in a ponderosa pine overhead. I've learned through years of studying owls not to ignore owl omens. So I established my camp nearby, and when I woke up the following morning, the owls were still perched in the pines, watching me.

Most every world culture, during some period of its development, has revered owls as bearers of wisdom or feared them as conjurers and messengers from the other side. Traditional Ojibwa stories describe how the souls of the dead must pass over an "owl-bridge" to reach the spirit world. The Northwest Coast Indians say that a hooting owl portends death. The Cheyenne word *mistae* denotes both "spirit" and "owl."

The scientific name for the burrowing owl, *Athene cunicularia*, derives from the Greek goddess of wisdom, Athena, who carried a small owl on her arm. Lakota warriors carried burrowing owls into battle, believing the owls' strong medicine would repel enemy arrows.

A few years ago, archaeologists discovered a quarter-million-year-old human burial site deep in a cave in South Africa. They knew it had to be a burial site because virtually all the thousands of bones found in the cave were those of humans, except for one set: the skeleton of a little owl. It's easy to imagine the mourners taking this owl hundreds of feet down into the cave so it could serve as a spirit guide to the other world. Or maybe the little owl chose them.

Today, many of us tend to characterize belief in spirit guides as quaint superstition. However, anyone who has worked with owls will tell you that their aura of omniscience is well-earned. Owls show wisdom in the way they calmly watch us, materializing and vanishing at will. As top-rung predators endowed with supersensitive sight and hearing, they quietly take command of their surroundings, seeming self-composed and aloof. And for whatever reason, we seem to become aware of them during times of grief.

Many of us have heard stories of owls visiting a friend or relative after the death of a loved one. When I told a close friend about the spotted owls visiting our backyard patio after my mother's death, she said yes, the same thing had happened to her after her mother died. She had gone walking alone in the Ohio woods, and a barred owl had flown up and perched on a branch above her.

Another friend told of the time her one-year-old son was dying of heart failure in a Los Angeles hospital. That evening a "white owl" (probably a barn owl) flew in and perched on the window ledge outside his room. The next morning the boy's vital signs had strengthened, and twenty years later, he leads a normal life.

Since I began studying owls more than forty years ago, they have visited me time and again, especially when I'm alone or feeling sad. I remember the tiny flammulated owl who hooted beside my tent at tree line in Colorado's Indian Peaks Wilderness; the northern saw-whet who caressed my hair with his talons in the Boulder Mountain Park; and the great horned owl who joined me one frigid night along Nebraska's North Platte River, perching eight feet away on a bare cottonwood limb as a fiery comet flared across the sky.

Each of these encounters left me more alert, more receptive of nature's gifts, and happier to be alive. Owls seem to provide a link between us and nature. Quietly waiting for them, gazing into their glowing eyes, or hearing their soothing voices at night leaves us feeling more tuned in to everything around us.

So when I heard those owls hooting above my tent at Pine Lake and found them there again at dawn, silently watching, I decided to stay another night. I kept coming back, and over thirty-five years of visiting through all the seasons, I grew to know the lake and its environs better than any other place on earth.

October is the most likely time to see or hear owls at the lake. First, there are more of them, since the year's young are still around begging for morsels from their parents. Courtship has already begun, so it's not uncommon to hear three or more species hooting at dusk and dawn.

Great horned owls nest in the pines on the west and north sides of the lake, and each evening their booming voices let everyone know who's in charge. Eastern screech-owls lay their eggs in natural cavities in cottonwoods at the north end of the lake, wailing and warbling out their territorial calls from October through July. I've heard the steam-engine-like hiss of barn owls in the pine woods, watched agile short-eared owls course over the cattail marshes, and seen a family of burrowing owls bobbing up and down in a ground squirrel colony near the bobolink meadow.

But one thing I've learned from owls is not to go looking for them. Plains Indians have talked of this. A Lakota friend once told me I was crazy to go out at night playing tape-recorded owl calls in hopes of attracting owls. "You don't want to do that," she said, implying that such brazenness was tantamount to opening the door to Death and inviting him in for dinner.

As a naturalist, I learned the lesson in a subtler way. I found that when I went deliberately looking for owls, especially if I was leading a class or field trip, the owls typically showed little interest in revealing themselves. On the other hand, if I sat quietly in the woods, minding my own business, the owls sometimes came to me. That was the first lesson they taught me, and it has served me well over the years as I've struggled to quiet my neurotic human impulses to seek, find, and accomplish.

I'd like to say I wasn't obsessing about owls that October evening as I strolled around the north end of the lake in the moonlight. However, it would have been impossible to ignore them. Both pairs of great horned owls were hooting away on either side of the lake, the males' basso "who-whoo, whoo-whooo" synchronizing with the higher pitched "who-wh-wh-whoo, wh-who-whoo" of their mates. At intervals, one of the youngsters would throw in a falsetto version of its parents' calls.

As I walked by a small grove of cottonwoods, a screech-owl concealed in a nearby red cedar let loose a series of tremulous whinnies, and its mate answered from deeper in the woods. I stopped there and stood facing southeast toward the full moon, feeling its cold canescent light flow through me and listening to the chinks and rasps of red-winged blackbirds in the marsh. I didn't hear the screech-owls again, but when I returned to camp and climbed into my frosty tent, the great horns were still hooting away.

Sometime after midnight, an eerily familiar call nudged me awake. When I realized what it was, I bolted upright in my sleeping bag and cupped my hands behind my ears to amplify the sound.

"Hoooo" (on one pitch).

"Hoooouuuuu" (descending like a sigh).

"Hoooo."

"Hoooouuuuu."

"Hoooo."

"Hoooouuuuu."

I couldn't believe it. I'd heard the poignant courtship duet of long-eared owls on CDs but never in the wild. I closed my eyes and took it all in—the male's rhythmic, mellifluous hoots, the female's lilting replies, the rise and fall of their hollow voices in the crisp night air.

During my first fifteen years of camping out at the lake, I'd seen or heard long-ears only twice. The first time was in 1990, when my friend Roger had inadvertently begun to erect his tent under an old crow nest containing an incubating long-ear. Roger moved his tent, but I still feared that this nesting attempt would fail, for other reasons. Sure enough, when I returned to the spot two months later, I found an empty nest with a family of great horned owls gathered in the pines around it.

In fact, I had never expected to find any long-eared owls at Pine Lake. These medium-sized, rusty-feathered conjurers have disappeared from much of the prairie region. They suffer from human disturbance of dense thickets, where they nest, and con- version of wet meadows, where they hunt mice and voles, to hay meadows. The proliferation of human-adapted great horned owls poses a daunting threat. These larger, more aggressive owls have followed European Americans across the continent, competing with the long-ears and preying on them.

Invasive American crows provide convenient used nests for the long-ears, but they knock the young out of the nests and eat them. In a poignant way, long-eared owls have become a barometer of our stewardship of the western prairies; wherever humans gather in numbers or carve up the landscape, these owls tend to disappear.

While becoming rare on the Great Plains, long-eared owls actu- ally thrive in some parts of North America, particularly where foli- age grows dense enough to protect them from larger owls. They range clear across the United States and southern Canada, as well as through Europe, northern Asia, and parts of North Africa. Named for the false "ear" tufts that sprout from the top of their head, these owls also possess a distinctly squarish, rusty facial disk. This disk helps to channel sound to their large, sensitive ears, actually located on the sides of the head.

Standing just over a foot tall but with wingspans of three feet or more, these acrobatic predators hunt while darting through woodland thickets or coursing low over open meadows. They often catch their prey by "stalling out" and dropping straight down. Though quiet and reclusive, long-ears can grow fierce when defending a nest. In *Life Histories of North American Birds of Prey*, naturalist Arthur Cleveland Bent wrote: "I know of no bird that is bolder or more demonstrative in the defense of its young, or one that can threaten the intruder with more grotesque performances or more weird and varied cries."

After that initial sighting in 1990, I hadn't encountered another long-ear at the lake for several years, until one June night when I was out hiking after midnight and detected a synthesizer-like wail deep in the woods. I followed the sound through the trees, occasionally tripping over logs or bumping into low-hanging limbs, until I found myself kneeling in the sand on the edge of the woods as the screaming ebbed away.

That was it. As things appeared to have been changing slightly for the worse at the lake—more pheasants, European starlings, rock doves, and other invasive birds; fewer native curlews and sharp-tailed grouse—I assumed the long-ears had little chance of holding on.

This ongoing unraveling of the earth's natural systems—even out here amid twenty thousand square miles of mostly natural prairie—leaves a hollow feeling in the pit of the stomach, a sense of dread inevitability. So, though I'd continued to think about these attractive and secretive owls and sometimes listened for their calls, I'd held out little hope of seeing them again.

Under those circumstances, this October's moonlight serenade felt like more than a gift. It offered a spark of hope, an affirmation of persevering wildness at the lake. I sat shivering in my sleeping bag and reveled in those ancient sounds, savoring each note, trying to wrap myself in the music, inhale it, absorb it.

"Hoooo."

"Hoooouuuuu."

"Hoooo."

"Hoooouuuuu."

"Hoooo."

"Hoooouuuuu."

After awhile I began to realize that I knew those calls intimately, not from recordings but deep in my gut, and that knowledge surely evolved out of millions of years of waiting and listening in the darkened woods. I thought of my ancestors in Africa and Eurasia, sitting around a blazing fire, trying to make sense of those otherworldly sounds. I thought of the owls, courting like this and rearing their young in humid woodlands populated by mammoths and saber-toothed cats, cooing and courting through the ice ages, the evolution of the North American prairie, the coming and going of diverse human cultures.

I thought of the millions of years it had taken for long-eared owls to develop their startling array of vocalizations, including barks, wails, and squawks of alarm; kazoo-like squeals around the nest; single hoots used to advertise nesting territories; and this rare, exquisite duet. I thought of how these secretive owls, sensitive to the presence of the always alert and much larger great horned owls, often avoid vocalizing at all.

This pair seemed oblivious to potential dangers as they called deep into the night.

"Hoooo."

"Hoooouuuuu."

"Hoooo."

"Hoooouuuuu."

"Hoooo."

"Hoooouuuuu."

The persistence and synchronicity of the duet suggested the owls were serious about nesting, probably in the dense thicket of pines and red cedars just north of my tent. They called again the following night. But I never saw them. I hardly looked for them at all, feeling content to imagine their silhouetted forms perching alertly in the shadows, two pairs of golden irises blazing in the starlight as the pair hooted out their desire for sustaining life.

Feather's Touch

I rarely take friends with me to the Sandhills. It's not that I don't like company. I love walking in the woods with quiet companions, and my teaching and consulting work involves going out into the field with groups of students and volunteers. But we all long for sanctuaries, sacred places we hold close to our hearts that call to be experienced alone.

Nevertheless, when my close friend Chris said he'd like to join me on one of my camping trips, I didn't hesitate to invite him. Tall, broad shouldered, and appearing at least a decade younger than his seventy-three years, Chris is a practicing Buddhist and eco-psychologist who writes books of poetry and prose celebrating our spiritual relationship with nature. When I bumped into him at a friend's art show twenty years ago, the first things I noticed were his eager smile, his oversized, 1980s-style eyeglasses, his Beatle-length haircut, and a bear claw dangling from a rawhide cord around his neck.

In *The Hoop and the Tree,* Chris describes how nearly all world religions use tree symbolism to express our longing to draw from family and spiritual roots and reach toward the divine. We use hoop symbolism to express our need for circles of community, including family, friends, and nature. The book resonates with astute and sometimes sardonic comments on human existence. At one point he notes, "Given the current state of the world, if you're not depressed, there's something wrong with you." But then he shares an array of peaceful pathways toward wholeness and community.

We've often talked about the joys of spending quiet time alone with nature, so I knew Chris would understand my need to disappear periodically during our three days in the Sandhills. I also knew that he would love Pine Lake, if only because he understood what the place meant to me.

We drove to Oshkosh and took the country road north through Crescent Lake National Wildlife Refuge. Twenty miles north of the Platte River valley, the road narrows to a one-lane ribbon of crumbling asphalt that rises and falls over the dunes and serpentines through lush wetlands and fragrant hay meadows. Generally the preponderance of the "traffic" consists of bull snakes, box turtles, or a few cows and calves loitering in the middle of the road.

Once within the wildlife refuge, the road meanders around a dozen shallow lakes and ponds, each with a slightly different character. Island Lake stretches a mile across, with big rafts of ducks and geese out in the middle and floating nests of eared grebes along shore. Smaller Gimlet Lake sports a cormorant nesting colony in ghostly white cottonwood snags, a family of trumpeter swans, and head-high stands of native tallgrass prairie. White-tailed deer bound through marshes and willow thickets between Gimlet and Roundup Lakes, and shorebirds crowd into shallow ponds on either side of the road.

We turned onto a sand trail (a local term for a primitive, two-track road) and stopped at Crane Lake, a brackish, half-mile-wide body of water tucked into soft green hills. No sooner had we jumped out of the car than Chris looked around, then at me, his face glowing.

"Oh Steve, thank you for bringing me to this place."

I showed Chris a bald eagle nest in a big cottonwood across the water, and we walked along a sand trail framed by blooming yuccas and trumpet gilia, stopping to examine the occasional grasshopper or dung beetle. An ornate box turtle lumbered across the trail and waddled into a clump of golden switchgrass, while a family of mule deer watched us curiously from a distant dune.

We shared a simple lunch of crackers, cheese, fruit, and tea while leaning against the car and admiring a flock of white-faced ibis who had settled down in the mudflats along the near shore. A half dozen black terns dipped and dove over the water as we climbed back into the car and drove north.

While bouncing along the pothole-strewn road, we talked about sacred places. Chris told me of some of his favorite hideouts in the Utah desert, narrow slot canyons with salmon-colored cliffs and cool grottos where silvery droplets of rainwater trickle into still pools. He described one of these places as a living cathedral, with constantly changing, glowing light.

"For me, sacred places are places in nature where you feel a sense of a presence of something bigger, a sense of being part of something bigger than yourself."

Chris and I agreed that the sacredness of each place comes as much from the attitude of the beholder as from the location's physical attributes. Chris referred me to Ian Baker's *The Heart of the World*, a book about searching for lost Edens in the Tibetan Himalayas. In the book's introduction, the Dalai Lama writes: "In the Buddhist tradition, the goal of pilgrimage is not so much to reach a particular destination as to awaken within oneself the qualities and energies of the sacred site, which ultimately lie within our own minds."

We agreed, though, that natural, untrammeled landscapes offer greater opportunities for immersion in nature and spirit.

"A sacred place could be a tree in your backyard or a small park in your neighborhood, if you approach it with the right state of mind," said Chris. "We all need intimate contact with nature. It's part of our genetic code, our inner being."

We arrived at Pine Lake in midafternoon, and after setting up camp, I excused myself to spend some time in the woods reading while Chris explored the lakeshore on his own. I stretched out in the pine needles on a sandy slope near camp, just above the pine and juniper thicket where I'd heard the long-eared owls calling the previous October. After a half hour or so the soft breeze and sweet pine scent achieved their soporific effect, and I drifted off.

I awoke to a rustling sound in one of the larger pines downslope from me. A ball of rust-colored feathers poked out from behind a clump of needles, then an owlish head with two small ear tufts. The tufts were so short that I first mistook the owl for a fledgling great horned, but it was far too small. It had to be a young long-ear fresh off the nest.

The owl struggled onto a sturdy limb and rested there in the sun. I gazed its way for a few minutes, then picked up my book and tried to read. After awhile a flash of movement caught my eye, and I looked up just as the owl took flight and glided straight toward me. I held my breath as she flared her wings and landed on a bare branch ten feet above my head.

To see a long-eared owl that close—her delicate, rufous feathers ruffling in the breeze, her tawny head turreting around, her round yellow eyes peering intently down—seemed too miraculous to believe. I talked to the young owl in the most soothing tones I could muster, saying how pleased I was to see her, how handsome she looked on her shaded perch. The owl hardly reacted at all, resting there serenely while swiveling her head all the way around and back.

We shared that quiet space in the woods for an hour or so, until the fledgling sailed off to the south and vanished into a thicket of scrawny pines. An outburst of squawks and squeals as she hopped around in the foliage suggested that she had company. I eventually counted three long-eared owls in there, one adult and two young.

I found Chris sitting at a picnic table down by the lakeshore. Breathless with excitement, I told him about the owls and asked if he'd like to see them.

"Absolutely," he said.

We sneaked back to the big tree and sat down together. The owls went ballistic. With frightened squawks and barks, they exploded from the pine thicket and flapped wildly away to the south. Stupid human. I should have realized they wouldn't recognize or trust my friend.

I apologized to the owls, and then to Chris, before the two of us circled sheepishly back through the pines to the picnic area.

I didn't return to the lake until October, five months later. I arrived late on a blustery evening, pitched my tent in the usual spot, and went right to sleep.

I had an assignment for the next morning. Chris and his friend Peter had been shepherding their respective sons through adolescence. As part of the process, they'd set up a "council of elders" to get together every other month with the boys to sit around a bonfire, eat pizza, and explore various coming-of-age issues. The group's current assignment was to go off somewhere alone and spend a couple of hours sitting quietly observing nature. We were to bring back something from the experience to share with the group.

I rose an hour before sunrise, walked over to my quiet spot in the woods, and sat there meditating as the pink glow of false dawn tinted the eastern sky. Just as the silhouettes of the trees had begun to resolve in the gray light, a long-eared owl glided by, nearly brushing my face with its silent wings.

I spent the rest of the day wandering around the lake and over the dunes. Juniper solitaires (*Myadestes townsendi*—see the notes section for other common names), newly arrived from the north, had converged on the woods and were already warbling out their winter songs, used to stake out and defend junipers loaded with purple berries.

I saw the white-tailed doe and her two fawns bounding through the cattail marsh at the north end of the lake and flushed a small flock of sharp-tailed grouse in the adjacent dunes. I sat on one of the highest dune crests soaking up the sun while chattering flocks of red-winged blackbirds flared overhead.

That evening I stood on the west shore of the lake as the sinking sun set the golden cottonwoods and burgundy-tinted prairie on fire. Groups of white pelicans and cormorants creased the placid water, while tiny emerald-green damselflies floated from one cattail stalk to another. I heard a ripple in the blue, a rolling, pulsating call, and located a flock of several hundred sandhill cranes circling high overhead. The trumpeting intensified as the cranes scrambled into ragged waves and sailed south.

After sunset the coyote families exchanged yips, and the owls began vocalizing from all directions. I counted nine calling individuals—four great horned owls and two eastern screech-owls along the lakeshore and three squawking long-ears behind my tent. I wandered up that way and lay down in the pine needles, gazing up at the indigo sky.

An owl barked, off to my left. I hooted twice, very softly. The owl responded with shy barks and wails. I hooted again and the owl wailed back. I wasn't sure what to make of this exchange, but every time I hooted, the owl responded, and we conversed in that manner until the cold night air settled in and the last daylight drained away from the woods.

Suddenly two of the owls hung overhead, fluttering like giant bats. I could just discern the silhouettes of their round heads twisting around to peer down at me as their wings flailed, struggling against gravity. I felt the heat of their eyes, probing and questioning.

They hovered there for a second or two, nearly within reach, then vanished. All the stars came out and the ponderosas began to shiver and sway. I snuggled up in my sleeping bag and drifted off to the creak and groan of the trees, the rush of the wind, and the calls of hunting long-eared owls.

When I awoke at dawn, a dense fog had enveloped the lake and woods, softening the contours of the dunes, amplifying the cries of the wild geese, coating the bending grasses with droplets of glistening dew. In this fresh-made, eiderdown world, each breath felt like a caress, each footstep, a precious gift.

Ojo de Agua

Sandhills rain has a lightness of touch that complements the softness of the rolling landscape. There's no gurgle or roar, just a steady hiss as the raindrops caress the grass and trickle into the sand. Hardly a trace of rain remains on the ground. Like giant sponges, the dunes sop up the heavenly bounty, holding it just long enough for the deep-rooted grasses to absorb the moisture they need to survive the inevitable days of searing heat and desiccating wind.

Over a period of days or weeks, the untapped water percolates down through the dunes until it accumulates in a two-hundred- to nine-hundred-foot-thick layer of consolidated sands and gravels. This sandstone complex, known as the High Plains (or Ogallala) aquifer, extends from North Dakota to Texas and holds more water than Lake Huron. At least half of the water in the aquifer lies under the Nebraska Sandhills.

Much of the water in the aquifer accumulated during the Ice Age and is being depleted by irrigation. High Plains farmers pump billions of gallons of water out of the aquifer each day. In areas of southwestern Kansas and northern Texas, groundwater levels have dropped as much as two hundred feet in fifty years.

Not so in the Sandhills. Here the sandy soil makes cultivation challenging, and groundwater levels have remained relatively stable, fluctuating only a few feet up or down during wet or dry weather cycles. Throughout the Sandhills, the water often lies so close to the surface that its imprint speckles the landscape with a network of shallow ponds, cattail marshes, fens, and sedge-rush meadows.

As the immense reservoir of water creeps eastward beneath the dunes, it runs up against underground faults and impermeable rock layers and surges to the surface, bursting out in artesian springs. One bubbling spring on the banks of the Dismal River, known among locals as the Blue Pool, measures twenty-five feet across. Divers with sounding equipment have explored its depths, penetrating more than one hundred feet down into the aquifer.

The near constant flow of spring water enables rivers and creeks throughout the Sandhills to flow at even rates and within narrow temperature ranges throughout the year. That's one reason why river otters, trumpeter swans, and sixty native fish species thrive in this improbable landscape.

For Sandhills ranchers, the artesian springs provide a reliable source of water for cattle and horses. For the romantic and earth centered, the springs represent much more. Denise Sammons, who grew up in the Sandhills before migrating east to study hydrology, writes:

> As a child, it was nothing short of magical . . . the elixir of princesses and wizards, the fountain of youth sought by conquistadors. Later, I simply took it for granted as the most available thirst-quencher on a hot day. It bubbled from fountains near my two-room schoolhouse, gushed from spouts over horse tanks and sustained farm ponds dotting the countryside. But when my life led me away to the city, I mourned its absence and carried it off by the jugfull from my visits home. No water on earth could compare to the cold, clear, fresh-flowing artesian well water of my youth.

It's hard to think of a more alluring image in nature than clear, cold water bubbling out of the ground. I remember a trip with my parents to Mount Shasta, in Northern California, when I was ten. While driving up the mountain, we passed a sign that read, "Headwaters of the Sacramento River, 1.2 miles." I couldn't imagine actually witnessing the source of a major river, and I begged my father, who was usually good for just about anything, to stop so we could hike up to the spring.

When we arrived at the spot, we found a foot-wide brook emerging from under a mossy ledge and tumbling down a verdant hillside. These waters would feed the mighty Sacramento, then join the Pacific Ocean, then rise up into stratus and cumulus clouds that swirl eastward over the Cascade Mountains, then return to the earth as the cleansing rain that replenishes the aquifer under the mountain and feeds this perfect little spring. It all seemed too miraculous to believe. I wanted to crawl inside and wrap myself up in the wonder of it all.

What I didn't know at the time was that this spring is considered sacred by the people who have lived around Mt. Shasta for thousands of years.

Like indigenous peoples living around Mount Shasta, my Celtic ancestors venerated the springs that bubble up from down below, in the fertile otherworld, and they used the sacred spring water to cure ailments and weave magic. Young women wishing to become pregnant placed egg-shaped rocks, called serpent's or dinosaur eggs, around the mouths of oceanside springs and built vagina-shaped rock enclosures around the openings so that the salty, frothy seawater would flow in. Young chieftains sometimes strengthened their power by mating with the "keeper of the well," often a young woman appearing in the form of a white swan.

Some springs were considered treacherous. "Eye wells" could cure blindness and instill knowledge, but they could also take the sight of those who stared too intently into them. One spring, known as the "Well of Segais," was celebrated as a font of knowledge and the source of Ireland's seven sacred rivers.

Across the western plains of North America, indigenous peoples camped around sacred springs and adorned them with rock art. In southeastern Colorado archaic hunters carved images of connecting circles and stylized game animals onto ocher sandstones overhanging seeps and springs. Later, Apache and Comanche artists inscribed these same cliffs with pictures of bison, serpents, sun-like spirals, and rainbows.

The Pawnees, who built their earth lodges in the Sandhills along the three forks of the Loup River, tell how the artesian springs feeding these rivers serve as portals to an underground world. All the animal lodges gather down there in the darkness: the beavers and bobcats, wolves and coyotes, turtles, frogs, and water snakes. If you sit by one of these springs, you can see the kingfisher diving headfirst through the water, carrying messages from the beings above to the beings below.

A traditional Pawnee story, recounted by George Dorsey in *Pawnee Mythology*, tells of a time long ago when the people were poor and starving. A young man climbed up to a hill overlooking a cave spring and spent several days crying out to the spirits. On the second evening, he became mesmerized by the image of the full moon in the pool below the spring. When he waded out toward the reflection, he saw the face of an old woman. She told him to go back up to the top of the hill and cry all night.

The following evening, he descended the hill to drink from the spring, and when he looked up he saw a young girl sitting at the mouth of the cave. She transformed into the old woman he'd seen the night before and then vanished into the cave.

He followed her in, where he found another country, with grassy hills and clear rivers flowing in every direction. They sat down together and Mother Moon instructed him in ways to build earth lodges, plant and harvest corn, and hunt bison. She told him the bison would soon come if the people were patient.

Then one day the small opening of the cave trembled, and throngs of bison came rumbling out onto the prairie. Because Mother Moon had instructed the people in the proper way of hunting and honoring the bison, the herds kept coming, replenishing the animals who were killed. From that time on, the people lived well.

In its own way, Pine Lake comprises one big "eye of water" that reflects the infinite depth of life above, in the clouds and heavens, and reveals the mysteries of life below, in the womb-like calm of the High Plains aquifer.

The small creek that feeds the lake, nourished by waters that mound up beneath the dunes, seeps into a natural basin crowded with cattails and bulrushes, where bitterns and mink come to forage and rear their young.

The year after I got to know the long-eared owls, I decided to camp beside this giant seep during the first full moon of each season and sit alone in the surrounding dunes, waiting for whatever might come my way. During the Sore Eyes Moon—March in the modern European calendar—I arrived just as the shimmering orb cleared the somber, snow-flecked hills to the east. I pitched my tent in the moon shadow cast by a small grove of ponderosas fifty yards up from the edge of the marsh.

As I was organizing camp, a great horned owl flushed from one of the pines and circled out over the dunes with a raucous family of crows in hot pursuit. Down below me, hundreds of duck silhouettes glided across golden splashes of moonlight on the water.

I could hear their voices—the nasal quacks of mallards; "come here" whistles of American wigeons; imperious grunts of gadwalls; "tuk, tuk" calls of northern shovelers; peacock-like wails of redheads; clucks and cackles of canvasbacks, coots, and mergansers. Every once in a while I'd sense the earthquake-like rumble of whirring wings—probably a bald eagle or osprey startling them but too dark now to see.

I sat propped up against a ponderosa eating a makeshift supper of dark chocolate and tangerines while soaking in the potpourri of spring sounds, until the north wind came up strong, tossing the pine boughs and nearly ripping my tent loose from its moorings. I staked it back down and crawled in, falling asleep to the rush of the wind and the keening wails of a family of coyotes just up the hill.

When I crawled out of the tent at dawn, my water bottle was frozen solid, and the sun struggled to burn through an icy, blowing fog. The dune sand felt hard as cement. Even the usually soft pocket gopher mounds had petrified. The sun rode free of the swirling clouds for a few minutes, and I stood on a dune crest soaking up each precious ray.

I knew this wouldn't last. The sun and the aquifer conspire to create their own weather, a mélange of penetrating humidity and swirling wind more reminiscent of Wales than the Great Plains. As soon as the sun rises, its warmth begins to stir up the supersaturated layer of air over the water, and when that layer encounters even colder air a few hundred feet up, the fog reforms. By the time I had crunched my way through the ice-encrusted switchgrass bordering the marsh, the low clouds had swallowed up the sun.

I stood where the tallgrass prairie meets the cattails, stamping my feet to ward off frostbite, listening to the quacking, whistling, rasping, wheezing, and honking. I could see a few hundred ducks and geese. The rest seemed to be holed up in small pockets of open water surrounded by acres of eight-foot-high cattails.

I walked south a few hundred yards until I found a sickle-shaped peninsula of grass that extended into the heart of the marsh. From this last point of semidry land, nearly surrounded by cattails and water, I could hear the subdued gurgling and muttering of ducks and geese in a concealed opening about fifty yards away. I guessed there might be several dozen in there waiting to fly out.

After a few minutes their conversation rose in inflection and energy, like the swelling murmurs in a crowded concert hall just before the conductor takes stage. The sun popped out of the racing clouds, and the first flock took flight. They emerged to my left, a couple hundred Canada geese who skimmed over the water, then honked excitedly and banked to the right as they fought their way north against the wind.

A second flock of several hundred ducks and geese burst out, then more flocks, then smaller groups of whirring pintails and whistling wigeons. Like clowns clambering out of a Volkswagen Beetle, the ducks and geese continued to squeeze out of the marsh. Every time I concluded that the cattails held no more birds, another flock raised its voice and streamed forth.

At long last I heard several high, tinny exclamations, like toy trumpets, and here they came, two snow-white trumpeter swans, flying wingtip to wingtip with their necks stretched out against the north wind. They passed overhead, and I could see their triangular, black bills, confirmation that they were indeed trumpeters.

I remembered the Irish legends in which the Keeper of the Well often appears in the guise of a swan. The earth goddess had outdone herself here, creating this silent passageway from the dark aquifer, where the upwelling waters melt away the winter ice and provide nutrients for thousands of early migrating waterfowl.

As I turned away from the marsh, little pieces of the sky appeared to break loose and tumble down, alighting on a line of wooden fence posts: bluebirds, twenty-five rusty-and-blue easterns, and a single cerulean mountain. They perched on the posts long enough to afford good viewing through binoculars. Their restless fluttering and preening betrayed the nature of their migratory agenda, and within a few seconds they had lifted off and scattered north, trading exultant calls:

Fee-feww, fee-feww; fee-fee-feww. "Rejoice, rejoice, spring at last."

I wanted to know what was feeding all the ducks, geese, and swans, so I extracted an empty yogurt container from my pack, walked back down to the marsh, kicked a hole in the veneer of ice, and scooped up a half pint of spring water. Back at camp I poured some of the sacred elixir into an empty Sucrets container and went to work with a hand lens.

The water, which at first glance appeared clear, actually contained a scattered mix of marsh flora and fauna: arrow-shaped leaves of watermelon-green pondweed, cellophane-noodle strands of algae, nutty brown cattail seeds, spiny buffalo burs, and a few tiny but ferocious-looking dragonfly nymphs. Some even smaller creatures darted around, ricocheting like pinballs off the side of the container.

After boosting the magnification, I discerned a half dozen water fleas, one dark brown and resembling an embryonic vole with antennae, the others silver-green and nearly transparent. A shrimp-like copepod finned its way past a microscopic rotifer, which resembled a jellyfish with pulsating guts and little rippling hairs.

Still, all these tidbits seemed like meager rations for thousands of ducks and geese, and I began to understand the high-stakes drama that was playing out in the marsh. These waterfowl comprise the first wave, the risk-taking vanguards who follow the melting ice northward to choice nesting sites in the prairie potholes of the Dakotas and southern Canada. Arriving early on the nesting grounds, they increase their chances of securing favored breeding sites while also running the risk of becoming malnourished.

The raucous honking and quacking filling the air on this cold March morning had less to do with the bounty in the marsh than with a restless urge to head north and breed. For the ducks and geese, the marsh provides a temporary safe haven, a place to avoid predators for a night or two and grab a couple of bites before pushing northward.

Why not nest right here? Recent studies suggest that breeding ducks fare poorly in the Sandhills. Apparently the bull snakes, coyotes, and raccoons get most of their eggs and young. Meanwhile, more than half of the prairie potholes in the Dakotas and southern Canada have been drained and plowed over. Warming global temperatures will likely contribute to the loss of even more wetlands.

As I reflected on these realities each morning, the dawn cacophony grew more plaintive and poignant, and I wondered how many of the birds would make it back with their young next fall. I watched with renewed engagement as the gray skeins embarked north against pewter skies. On the morning when I packed up and drove away, I began to miss those wild voices long before the flocks had faded from view.

When I returned to the marsh one misty morning in June, nearly all the waterfowl were gone. A lone wood duck winged by as I sloshed through the waist-high grass, and a couple of mallards paddled around in the shallows—nothing more. Paradoxically, when I scooped up some marsh water and examined it under the hand lens, I found the cold consommé I'd sampled in March had heated up into an eclectic stew.

Rotifers, freshwater shrimp, dragonfly nymphs, tadpoles, and small leeches wriggled and darted through the murk. The brew was thick with moss, algae, and various microscopic creatures.

Much of that latent energy, transferred miraculously into clouds of hatching insects, seemed to have been sucked up by the songbirds. Hundreds of yellowthroats, marsh wrens, swamp sparrows, and blackbirds whistled, chattered, and squawked in the cattails, some flying to and fro with their beaks chock-full of mosquitoes, midges, and grasshoppers.

"Konkeree, konkeree!" The red-wings flashed their crimson epaulets and raised their guttural voices to the sky, throwing in an occasional loud "chink" that sounded like a blacksmith striking iron.

"Ooaawwrrrgg—konk-konk-ka-ung!" Two dozen yellow-headed blackbirds crowded onto a cattail island, evoking images of strangulation victims crying out for help as they extended their saffron necks and rasped out their ear-jarring proclamations of fitness.

To my right and my left, two male marsh wrens skittered up and down on cattail stalks, chattering away.

"B-di-di-di-dit-bzzt-bzzt-bzzt!" proclaimed marsh wren number one, his bill dripping cattail fluff as he eyed the globe-like nest he'd been working on.

"B-di-di-di-dit-bzzt-bzzt-bzzt!" answered number two, cocking his tail and holding on tight as his perch swayed in the breeze.

"Zzz-z-z-z-z-z-zut!" from number one.

An answering "zzz-z-z-z-z-z-zut" from number two.

Then a grating "b-zzeet-zzeet-zzeet-zzeet!" and a harsh trill from each singer.

I'd read about song-dueling among marsh wrens in Don Kroodsma's masterful *The Singing Life of Birds*, but I'd never taken the time to absorb the nuances of this territorial ritual. During fifteen minutes of listening, I charted more than a dozen distinct vocalizations from each singer (Kroodsma writes that a typical western marsh wren repertoire exceeds one hundred). As often as not, a particular song from one wren seemed to prompt the identical song from the second singer.

No one knows precisely why songbirds swap vocalizations in this manner. Perhaps the males want to show prospective mates that they can sing just as well as their neighbors. Maybe it's a threat gesture, something along the lines of "I heard that song, and I can sing it too, so watch out!" Think "Dueling Banjos" in the movie *Deliverance*. But as Kroodsma notes in his book, to really understand the motives behind the singers we'd need to ask the females. Their choices of breeding partners determine which songs get passed along from generation to generation.

However intended, the song-dueling of dozens of wrens in the cattails created a frenetic, mind-buzzing spectacle. If we only knew what powered these little wrens, I thought, we'd soon solve the world energy crisis. But we do know. It's the aquifer, and all those wrigglers and darters in the primordial soup.

And then, as the sun poked out of the mist, I looked around and began to notice all the nuances of green: spring-green cattails, forest-green horsetails, yellow-green junegrass, hay-green timothy, aqua-green bluegrass, silky-green needle-and-thread grass, downy-green mullein. Against this lush palette, little splotches of contrasting color beckoned seductively.

I swished through dewy patches of wild rose, lavender spiderwort, yellow-orange puccoon, magenta vetch, and white yarrow. I paused to watch the blue-gray head of a heron periscope out of the cattails, while along the shore a ruddy-flanked white-tailed deer tiptoed through thickets of wild licorice.

About then I almost took the plunge, remembering childhood mornings spent burrowing through and rolling in wet meadow grass—creating forts and secret passageways, scavenging sow bugs and centipedes, growing intoxicated from those earthy smells. But I was already soaked from the waist down, so I settled for sitting on a dune top while the sun warmed my legs and feet. I looked down in the grass and saw a glistening blue-eyed darner dragonfly engaged in the same pastime.

That evening the full moon came up blood red. The Pawnees have named this first moon of summer the Rose Moon; the Ojibwas, Strawberry Moon. Let's call it green grass moon, pelican moon, box turtle moon, marsh wren moon, nighthawk moon, mosquito moon, wood tick moon, budding fruits moon, moon of sultry nights and fertile dreams. A big bold moon to illuminate the swaying pine where a great horned owl hooted in consonance with the rushing wind.

The ducks were back, great rafts of them cruising across the steel-blue surface of the lake. Their feathers glowed in the light of the setting sun as a big harvest moon rose up behind the yellow-leaved cottonwoods on the far shore.

Thirty or so redheads paddled along smartly, wheezing out their shrill calls as they overtook a larger flock of black-and-white ringnecks. Farther out, more than a hundred ruddies rode high in the water, white cheek patches gleaming and tails fully cocked. Several hundred teal, anonymously clad in muted brown nonbreeding plumage, slurped their way through the shallows along the far shore. American coots, an assortment of grebes, a small gang of cormorants, and three big white pelicans glided in and out of the duck flotilla.

But the energy of last spring had dissipated. Gone was the explosion of sound, the frantic pre-breeding excitement. The water birds seemed laid-back, almost complacent, as they cruised across the lake. When the local wood duck family flew by my tent at dusk, their whistling wings barely creased the still air.

The landscape seemed to have softened as well. The strengthening moonlight illuminated a tapestry of muted colors: russet cattails and tawny switchgrass grading into flaxen meadows of prairie sandreed, pale burgundy clumps of little bluestem where the dunes rose up to the east and west.

The soothing autumn pastels and flocks of waterfowl out on the lake obscured a disturbing truth. Little rain had fallen the previous summer, and the western Sandhills remained parched after nearly seven years of drought. The shallow ponds south of Pine Lake had drained to cracked mudscapes. The level of the aquifer had dropped a couple of feet during those seven years.

For millennia, the High Plains aquifer has "drought-proofed" the Sandhills. During the Dust Bowl years, when surrounding High Plains topsoils were scoured away by the wind, subirrigated meadows throughout the Sandhills remained green, and livestock production actually increased. Archaeologists have found artifacts of fishing and hunting camps, thousands of years old, around Sandhills lakes, evidence that High Plains peoples have long sought refuge and sustenance here, especially during times of drought.

I'd been reassuring myself that the current period was just another one of those dry stretches when the aquifer recedes a few feet before the rains return. After all, the last two summers had been relatively wet in the eastern Sandhills and in eastern Colorado. During the 1990s, the wettest decade on record, water from the aquifer had lapped over Sandhills roads, leaving some ranches isolated and bewildered cows standing ankle deep.

But what if the rains didn't return? Some global warming models predict a long-term pattern of reduced precipitation and increased evaporation on the western plains. Under those climatic conditions, the aquifer could easily drop another ten to fifteen feet. Trumpeter swans and bald eagles might disappear, along with most mink, muskrats, and herons. Wood lilies and prairie orchids would wilt away as fens and marshes morphed into sterile hay meadows. Grazing capacity would diminish, driving family ranchers out of business.

Other threats also loom, including the Keystone XL pipeline, slated to bring crude oil extracted from Alberta tar sands through the eastern Sandhills and down to the Gulf Coast. Sandhills residents, Native American leaders, environmental activists, and the Biden administration have worked together to stop it, pointing out that frequent leaks in a completed portion in southern Canada have already spilled millions of gallons of crude oil onto native grasslands. In the Sandhills, leaks of this magnitude could permanently contaminate the aquifer.

My greatest fear is that during a future drought crisis, Denver or the fracking industry will somehow purchase water rights and begin pumping Sandhills water to parched areas of the Colorado Front Range. That would nearly destroy this twenty-thousand-square-mile island of mostly intact prairie.

This eventuality may sound far-fetched, but the Southern Nevada Water Authority has been negotiating for years with the state of Utah to pump water from their desert aquifers to Las Vegas. Meanwhile, in defiance of hard-fought agreements with Wyoming and Nebraska, Colorado continues to propose additional dam projects along the South Platte River, funded, obscenely, by taxes on sports gambling. If completed, these new dams could lower flow rates enough to compromise or eliminate critical habitat for migrating Sandhill cranes in central Nebraska.

How do you measure the cost of such catastrophes? Begin with the toy-trumpet calls of white swans on a frosty March morning. Or a parade of fluffy wood duck chicks teetering on the edge of their nest cavity high in a lakeside cottonwood before plopping into the water. Or the soundless resonance of the immense aquifer trickling slowly eastward, pooling up beneath the dunes and seeping out into a moonlit marsh. Sacred gifts all, ours to nurture and cherish.

In the Celtic tradition, sacred pools sometimes harbor long-lost civilizations. They say that you can peer down into the dark waters of highland lakes and see shimmering lights, even hear children laughing and cathedral bells tolling. These apparitions lure travelers like siren songs, then suddenly vanish, causing inconsolable grief and longing.

The apparitions that haunt us today are not of lost civilizations but of lost ecosystems: lush Amazon rain forests, boundless African savannas, rippling tallgrass prairies. From time to time we exult in finding traces of these earthly wonders, only to see them snuffed out or despoiled by human greed. I can't shake the image shared by ecologist John Madson in *Where the Sky Began*: "My feelings for tallgrass prairie," he wrote, "are like those of a modern man fallen in love with the face in a faded tintype."

A little after midnight, the local coyote clan gathered around the tent and awakened me with an ear-splitting array of yelps and squeals. Later an eastern screech-owl perched in the crown of the nearest pine and wailed like a tortured spirit. I slipped on my headphones, fumbled around for the parabolic microphone, and went tripping through the night, roller-coastering along with her liquid obbligatos and quavering glissandos.

Her cries cut off abruptly, and I felt a dissonant ringing in my ears, then heard the whining wheels of a semitruck out on the highway to the east. Shivering as the early morning chill invaded the sleeping bag, I zipped it all the way up, buried my head inside, and lay there wondering what miracles, or disappointments, would reveal themselves in the coming dawn.

The Arapahos, who might have camped at this very spot 150 years ago, sometimes refer to the screech-owl as *méstahke*, meaning simply "spirit." Tonight this little owl haunted an unlikely habitat, a verdant oasis far out in the treeless hills, where pure water trickling from the aquifer beneath the dunes sustains the cottonwoods in which she nests. How she and her ancestors got here, we'll never know. How long she'll stay will depend on how long that water keeps bubbling up from the ground.

Dawn Chorus

I awake to a soft violet sky and the sonorous hoots of great horned owls in the shadowed pines. As I crawl out of the tent and lace up my boots, I hear the eastern screech-owls warbling out their ghost-like tremolos in the cottonwoods along the lakeshore.

Lemon-breasted western kingbirds cackle and chortle while spiraling up from their nest tree, then shoot down after interloping blackbirds and grackles. In the next cottonwood over, orchard orioles whistle contrapuntal songs. By the time the eastern horizon burns incendiary pink, marsh wrens fill the cattails with their buzzing, mechanical chatter.

With their complex, carefully orchestrated music, the birds celebrate a new awakening, offering renewed opportunities to mate, forage, and thrive. Their calling up of the dawn reminds me of Pawnee ritual, where elders would gather to pray up the sun. Pawnee shaman Thirussawichi, whose people lived in the Loup River valley a few miles east of here 150 years ago, described this practice during an 1888 interview reported by George Bird Grinnell in *Pawnee, Blackfoot, and Cheyenne*:

> We call to Mother Earth, who has been asleep and resting during the night. We ask her to awake, to move, to arise, for the signs of the Dawn are seen in the east and the breath of new life is here.
>
> Mother Earth hears the call; she moves, she awakes, she arises, she feels the breath of the new-born Dawn. The leaves and the grass stir; all things move with the breath of the new day; everywhere life is renewed.
>
> This is very mysterious; we are speaking of something very sacred, although it happens every day.

This dawn feels particularly exciting because it's the morning of my annual breeding bird survey at Pine Lake. For twenty-four years I've headed out before sunrise on the first or second Tuesday of June to count the birds from ten point-count stations scattered around the west side of the lake. I find something new each year while marveling at the richness and resilience of the lake's nesting bird population.

My first survey point lies right at the picnic table, so while sipping a cup of tea, I note all the birds within one hundred yards: a western wood-pewee and the chickadee pair directly overhead, three mallards and two western grebes cruising by on the magenta-tinted water, three wild turkeys skulking through the pines, a mourning dove cooing off in the distance, a hairy woodpecker hammering away on a cottonwood branch, an eastern kingbird, two tree swallows, two American robins, four red-winged black-birds, a common grackle, two brown-headed cowbirds, and an American goldfinch.

Adding in the marsh wrens, western kingbirds, orioles, and a sweet-singing common yellowthroat in the cattails, I end up with eighteen species and thirty-two individuals during ten minutes of observation at this one stop. And the sun has just begun to clear the horizon.

Each bird vocalization carries messages denoting the singer's fitness and intent. Among the songbirds, birds that acquire a variety of songs through listening and imitation, some phrases advertise nesting territories while others serenade potential mates. Within any given species, be it Baltimore oriole, song sparrow, or American goldfinch, each singer possesses a unique repertoire of cadences and melodies. Among the male singers (we now understand that many females sing as well), he who sings best mates most.

With our relatively weak sense of hearing, we take in just a fraction of the songs' beauty and complexity. A few years ago, I acquired a parabolic microphone, enabling students in my bird acoustics classes to put on headphones and actually begin to hear what the birds were saying.

When we listened to a meadowlark, we heard a dozen clear notes bursting forth like a frenzied aria. A single hermit thrush seemed to sing four distinct flute-like phrases simultaneously, initially fooling us into thinking we were hearing two birds performing in synchrony. It turns out that songbirds can create separate sounds on either side of their syrinx (a vibrating vocal organ at the base of the trachea), and that thrushes can also produce overtones, thus creating a four-part cadenza.

We also heard a puzzling background noise on some of our recordings. In the foothills of the Colorado Front Range, where a layer of airplane and automobile noise penetrates even the quietest canyons, the noise sounded low and rumbling; here in the Sandhills, it tended toward sweet and resonant. It took us a while to realize that we were sensing the pulse of nature—accumulated murmurs of distant birds, bees, crickets, cows, flowing water, and rustling leaves. This is the soothing music that accompanied our ancestors' daily lives and that few of us ever experience today.

At point two, on the edge of the cattail marsh near the south end of the lake, a half dozen male yellow-headed blackbirds sway back and forth on the cattail stalks, twisting their saffron necks skyward while issuing a dissonant mélange of rasps, gurgles, and groans. In their midst, a swamp sparrow perches on the spike of a cattail stalk, belting out his flat, trilling song.

Just to my right, seventeen cedar waxwings whistle their way into a thirty-foot-high crack willow anchored along the lakeshore. Named for the yellow and red, wax-like markings on their wings and tail tips, these stylishly crested denizens of open woods seemed uncommon at Pine Lake until about fifteen years ago. Now I find them munching on red cedar berries or perching in lakeside willows every spring. Farther along the shore, the harsh "wheeps" of a great crested flycatcher, an eastern woodland specialist, remind me that we're not on the unbroken prairie anymore.

At point three, located a little deeper into the marsh, the "oonk-a-loonk" of an American bittern, reminiscent of the sound made by a hand-operated water pump, oozes out from the cattails. These buff-colored herons sport vertical stripes that help them blend in among the cattails as they stand dead still with their beaks pointing skyward. They've declined throughout the western plains as agricultural activities have degraded natural wetlands and human-adapted predators have raided their ground nests. So it's always a relief to hear at least one calling along the lakeshore. Later, a high, descending squeal reveals a sora, a reclusive robin-sized rail, scurrying through the marsh.

From point three I walk westward, away from the lake and toward the dunes. As I enter a grassy meadow framed by fifty-foot-high ponderosa pines, I see a white-tailed doe standing one hundred yards away. I know this deer from previous encounters. This morning, instead of just watching me, she comes loping in my direction. I stand transfixed as she circles to within twenty feet, then walks up within shadow length, bowing down, stomping the ground with her hooves, and snorting out warnings.

It takes me a few seconds to realize that I'm actually being threatened by this three-foot-tall, delicate creature. It takes me another several seconds to understand why. It's early June, and she must have a newborn fawn lying out in the grass nearby.

I talk to her in soft tones, reassuring her that I have no interest in her fawn, and that I'm just passing through. She backs away a few feet, enabling me to swivel and head west into the hills.

For the next twenty minutes she stands in the meadow watching me. What on earth is this quiet two-leg doing in my meadow?

Point four lies at the crest of a dune two hundred yards west of the lake and feels like a different universe, with its swaying grasses, limitless vistas, and sense of quiet. The bustle of the marsh has faded away, and I can hear little more than a meadowlark warbling off in the grass and the chatter of eastern kingbirds and blackbirds ferrying grasshoppers from the dunes to their lakeside nests.

But what a view, with the grass-covered dunes underfoot, the glistening meadow where the doe stands quietly watching to the east, the lake and surrounding marsh and the soft green hills rolling and tumbling toward infinity. It's tempting to lie down in the soft grass and drift off in the fresh sunlight.

At point six, back in a cottonwood grove near the lakeshore, I find a house wren performing his explosive chattering song in a chokecherry thicket, exactly the same place where I've heard a house wren during nearly every one of my previous surveys. I've rarely encountered a singing house wren near any of my other nine survey points.

There's something here—probably a combination of dead trees with woodpecker holes for nesting and shrubbery loaded with insects—that creates the ideal breeding environment for this species. For me, it's like encountering an old friend, and it helps to confirm that the world is, indeed, an ordered and nurturing place.

Between points seven and eight, back along the lakeshore north of the picnic table, I stumble upon a breeding bird convention. First, a great crested flycatcher zips by with a green caterpillar wriggling in her beak and vanishes into a woodpecker hole. I can't hear the young cheeping, but I know they're in there.

In the same tree, a pair of European starlings brings insects to three gaping mouths protruding from another woodpecker hole. Overhead, eastern and western kingbirds flutter and dive as they compete for nesting space. Two male wood ducks fly by, their emerald green crests glistening in the morning sunlight.

All at once, the songbirds grow very quiet. I hear a harsh, woodpecker-like cackling and see a woodland hawk (*Accipiter cooperii*) glide in to one of the horizontal branches of a lakeside cottonwood.

The survey ends at point ten, located in the ponderosa pines just north of my tent site. Here I come across a singing northern mockingbird and warbling vireo and watch a red-breasted nuthatch stuff a caterpillar down the gullet of her fluttering fledgling. These observations bring the morning's total to sixty-four species.

Back at camp, I find a pair of blue jays scrounging scraps beneath the picnic table. Whenever I encounter jays looking for handouts, I recall my mother's endearing, if not "ecologically correct," relationship with her yard birds.

I was sitting in her living room sipping tea one morning and heard a "rat-a-tat-tat" on the patio door. I looked up into the coal black eyes of a western scrub-jay peering through the glass as Kay shuffled past me.

She opened the door and the scrub-jay hopped through the carpeted living room and into the kitchen, where he began plucking pieces of sourdough French bread off the green linoleum floor. I asked my mother if this happened often.

"Oh, he's pretty much a regular," she replied, with a hint of a smile.

I walked away smiling as well, even though I understood that this scrub-jay, along with an obese American crow who hung out on the patio, were probably wreaking havoc on native songbirds nesting in her backyard.

Bird lovers disparage these nest predators because they become dominant in human-altered landscapes, displacing other birds. We boost their numbers by fragmenting natural vegetation to the point where exposed songbird nests become easy pickings and by providing a smorgasbord of peanuts, garbage, and roadkill.

My breeding bird data suggest a modest decline in numbers of blue jays and crows at the lake over the past twenty-four years, with no more than three blue jays reported during any one survey. It feels reassuring to take an early morning walk in an environment where invasive, urban-adapted species are just one element in a thriving and diverse breeding bird population.

When I balance my one-burner stove on the creaky picnic table to brew a mug of coffee, the jays flap off toward the lakeshore. The songbird chorus begins to soften, and the cottonwoods shiver in the late-morning breeze as I stroll into the pines to spend some quiet time with the long-eared owls.

Over the years, I've documented 116 breeding bird species at Pine Lake. This richness stems from the variety of its ecosystems, including extensive cattail/bullrush marshes, mature cottonwood groves, thriving grasslands, and one of the largest ponderosa pine woodlands in the western Sandhills.

That's not to say that all this is natural. The cottonwoods have been encouraged by human stewardship, the ponderosas were originally planted by the generous ranch owners who eventually donated the land to Nebraska Game and Parks, and the grasslands have been shielded from grazing and natural fire.

Reviewing the breeding bird survey data over more than two decades, I notice an apparent decline in numbers of some grassland-nesting birds, including long-billed curlew and grasshopper sparrow. This is hardly surprising, given that grassland-nesting birds are considered the most threatened group in all of North America.

According to the North American Breeding Bird Survey, numbers of nesting grasshopper sparrows declined by two-thirds in the prairie region from 1966 to 2020, and curlews by nearly as much. Of the twenty-eight grassland-nesting birds tracked by this comprehensive survey, a dozen have shown declines of at least 2 percent per year.

The main cause appears to be habitat loss, with cornfields, oil and gas wells, subdivisions, and exotic woodlands replacing native prairies. In the Dakotas alone, more than ten million acres of grasslands were converted to GMO cornfields or soybeans during the first two decades of this century.

Broadcast-spraying of herbicides and pesticides on and around GMO crops has depleted insect populations that grassland birds depend on for food. A 2013–20 nationwide study coordinated by the Illinois College of Agricultural, Consumer, and Environmental Sciences concluded that for every 12 percent increase in use of neonicotinoid pesticides per county, populations of grassland-nesting birds declined by 2.2 percent.

But the apparent decline of curlews and grasshopper sparrows at Pine Lake may result from something entirely different, since grasslands within the wildlife area have been protected for several decades. Both these species breed most successfully in western prairies where clumps of knee-high grasses intersperse with shorter grasses and bare ground. They typically conceal their nests among the clumps of grass while foraging for grasshoppers and other insects in grass-free areas.

Prior to European conquest, modern bison grazed these grasslands for several thousand years, and lightning-caused or human-ignited fires periodically thinned out the dominant grasses, creating space for wildflowers and foraging room for nesting birds. By removing cattle from the grasslands surrounding Pine Lake, Nebraska Game and Parks may have created an area of prairie dominated by taller grasses and lacking the clumps of shorter grass that some grassland-nesting birds prefer.

In contrast, pasture-confined grazing on surrounding ranches, depending on its intensity and timing, may reduce habitat for birds that require tall grasses for nesting. Conversion of wet meadows to managed hay meadows inhibits nesting success of bobolinks and savannah sparrows, which are still incubating eggs or brooding young during early summer when hay is often cut. Seeing the combines rolling across these lush meadows while imagining what might lie beneath their whirling blades makes me shudder.

Natural disturbances are another matter. In Kansas's Konza Prairie, scientists have experimented with burning and/or grazing some grassland areas while completely excluding cattle and fire from others. Invariably, the areas burned and grazed support the highest diversity of plant and bird life.

In the Nebraska Sandhills, fires may burn hotter on windswept ridge tops, where they can scour away much of the native vegetation. But some birds, such as piping plover, nest in the bare sand these hot fires help create. Elsewhere, fires contribute to habitat richness by returning dead plant matter to the soil as ash, which stimulates regeneration of native grasses.

Most ecologists agree that optimal management for grassland-nesting birds should include a mix of rotational grazing and periodic burning, along with protecting active nest sites from human disturbance. In other words, the more our activities mimic natural and historic processes, the more our native species will prosper.

The most threatened grassland-nesting bird in the Sandhills could be the perky little piping plover, a plump, black-collared shorebird with a striking yellow-orange beak and orange legs. I've seen just one, a courageous adult who scurried back and forth between me and an apparent nest as I walked down the deserted road south of Crescent Lake.

On the western plains, piping plovers nest almost exclusively in areas of bare sand and gravel. Modern grazing practices, absence of fire, and loss of sandbars along the Platte River have eliminated most of their historic nesting habitat. Many of the remaining pairs in Nebraska have taken to nesting in sand quarries.

Ground-nesting birds face other threats in the Sandhills, including a proliferation of coyotes (whose numbers are no longer controlled by wolves), bull snakes, and other nest predators. A two-year study on private lands in the eastern Sandhills determined that thirty-eight mallard nesting attempts produced just a single surviving brood. Human-adapted predators appeared to have gotten most of the eggs or young on the other thirty-seven nests.

Historically, periodic fires killed off any trees that might invade this prairie. Now minions of eastern red cedars sweep in from the east and radiate out from human-created shelter belts, while deciduous trees proliferate along Sandhills streams and around lakes and ponds. At Pine Lake, I see more red cedars each year, with some beginning to sprout from the highest dunes.

These invasive trees provide dispersal corridors and breeding habitat for birds and mammals not previously found here, including some—such as fox squirrel, blue jay, American crow, and European starling—who feed on eggs and nestlings of native songbirds.

I noticed my first starlings at Pine Lake thirty years ago, when I watched a pair usurping a nesting cavity from a pair of red-headed woodpeckers. Now I see a few starlings every year and fewer of the woodpeckers.

But I wouldn't want to overemphasize these changes at Pine Lake. Not one of the species I found nesting here twenty-four years ago has disappeared, and only Eurasian collared-dove, great crested flycatcher, Bell's vireo, and great-tailed grackle—all birds that gravitate toward trees and shrubs—have been added to my list of nesting species since 2000. The average number of birds counted during my June breeding bird surveys hasn't changed appreciably.

This degree of bird population richness and stability seems remarkable, given all we hear about songbird decline throughout North America. Birdwatchers tend to pin these losses on a few widely publicized causes, such as insect die-off and global warming. These threats are very real and likely to become more impactful over time, but destruction of natural habitats by irresponsible land use is driving a large portion of the decline in native species populations we're observing right now. And much of bird mortality throughout North America stems from things we do in our daily lives that could easily be reversed.

These activities include leaving lights on in skyscrapers at night, which results in migrating birds becoming disoriented and crashing into the buildings by the hundreds of millions; allowing cats to roam freely, which results in the killing of more than a billion birds each year in the United States alone; and not holding government leaders accountable as suburban sprawl and industrial activities gobble up rural pastures and woodlands.

In areas of downtown Toronto and Chicago where skyscraper lights have been dimmed, bird mortalities have dropped 80 percent. In St. Louis, a consortium of nonprofits with only $30,000 of government support for their aggressive spay and neuter campaign appear to have reduced the feral cat population by a similar amount.

In the Dakotas, where new coal mines continue to scar the prairie, the Red Cloud Renewable Energy Center offers training and solar technology to Native American communities so they can reduce their use of fossil fuels. In some communities, household energy expenditures have been cut in half and carbon emissions have been reduced even more.

In the Nebraska Sandhills, federal protection of wetlands combined with sustainable grazing practices on private lands have helped maintain twenty thousand square miles of mostly native grassland where breeding birds continue to thrive. Here at Pine Lake, where the human footprint remains light, most of the native birds appear to be holding their own, at least for now.

Were I to climb up a giant beanstalk or an enchanted ponderosa pine, find myself in the sky, then look down at the lake through a porthole in the clouds, the image before me would appear almost identical to my first glimpse of this wondrous place thirty-five years ago. Any tears I might shed would emanate more from feelings of tenderness and familiarity than from pangs of loss.

Shorebirds in the Grass

While standing on a sun-washed dune just south of the campground the next morning, I hear a distinctive "kip-kip-kip" and look up just as a flock of brick-red and greenish-yellow birds scatters into the crown of a ponderosa pine. They must be crossbills, but what are these forest dwellers doing way out here?

Red crossbills wander hundreds of miles searching for bumper crops of conifer seeds. Their beak tips cross over, allowing them to insert the beaks between the conifer cone scales, pry the scales open by biting down hard, and then extract the seeds with their tongue. A single crossbill may harvest two thousand spruce seeds in a day, carrying three hundred at a time in its sublingual pouch.

Red crossbill populations have varying beak sizes and shapes, depending on which cone types they specialize in opening. Each of the eight identified beak types corresponds with a distinct repertoire of vocalizations, suggesting there might actually be eight separate species of "red crossbill." One new species has already been designated, the Cassia crossbill of the Idaho Rockies.

Crossbills that feed predominately on ponderosa pine cones typically possess the largest beaks. And they have exquisite voices, warbling out complex, sweet songs.

When crossbills find a bumper conifer cone crop, they'll cease their wanderings for a few months to nest and rear young, regardless of the time of year. A friend skiing in the Colorado Rockies in January once chanced upon a female, white-winged crossbill sitting serenely on her nest in a snow-flocked Engelmann spruce 10,400 feet above sea level!

A crossbill flock may fly from Canada to the southern Rockies searching for conifer seeds, "kipping" excitedly when they find a food source or prepare to depart from a seed-depleted tree. Their array of vocalizations also includes harsh, screaming distress calls; "tut-tut" alarm calls; and relatively soft "chitter" calls that help to keep the group together.

Over the millennia, crossbills and other conifer seedeaters have evolved a mutualistic relationship with firs, spruces, and pines. To control populations of seedeaters and guarantee that some of their seeds will ripen and germinate, conifers produce varying numbers of cones from year to year.

Some conifers, including Engelmann spruce and subalpine fir, synchronize their seed crops over enormous geographic areas. Remarkably, bumper seed crops of closely related spruces and firs can occur during the same year throughout both North American and Siberian boreal forests.

No one understands how the trees achieve this, whether by some kind of subtle communication through their root systems, through underground fungal networks that link the trees together, through spreading of pheromones and pollen, or by synchronous response to widespread environmental conditions.

Ponderosa pines, on the other hand, vary their seed production from stand to stand, so that within a relatively small geographic area some groves of pines will produce almost no cones during a given year while others abound with cones.

Crossbills that specialize in extracting ponderosa pine seeds fly from one forest area to another until they find cone-laden trees, feed voraciously for a few days or weeks, then move on. By carrying dozens of seeds in their sublingual pouches and dropping some of them here and there, these crossbills help to spread the trees they depend on.

And here is this clamoring flock, eighty miles from the nearest conifer forest, descending on this one-hundred-acre island of ponderosa pines way out on the prairie. Were they lured here by subtle cues produced by the pines, or is this isolated grove simply a regular stop on their habitual foraging route?

I sidle up their way, settle into the pine needles, and focus my binoculars. Overhead, a yellow-green female clings to the tip of a ponderosa branch, "kip-kipping" away. Right above her, two brick-red males dangle from separate cones, twisting their heads sideways as they insert their open beaks between the scales. I hear a scratching sound as they probe, crunch down, and extract seeds with their tongues.

The ponderosa resembles a giant Christmas tree, with twenty or more red and yellow-green crossbills ornamenting its branches and cones. The air resonates with "tut-tuts" and "kips" as flock members communicate their excitement. After a few minutes, the calls rise in intensity, followed by a flutter of wings and silence.

The flock roller-coasters away, toward another grove of pines a couple of hundred yards to the south. I reach down and pick up one of the bronze cones, pricking my index finger on its sharp spines while trying to pry open the scales. I finally manage to remove a papery sheath, about an inch long, with a seed smaller than a grain of rice embedded in its tip.

I place the seed on my tongue and savor its piney flavor. But what a chore to extract just one, and imagine having to extract several hundred per day. And all that chattering and flying energy expended in the process. Survival in nature seems a pretty tenuous proposition.

Off to the northwest another rich, finch-like song bursts from a grove of junipers at the woodland edge. No problem identifying this sound; juniper solitaires (*Myadestes townsendi*) also fly out to the prairie from the Rocky Mountains but to feed on juniper (known in Nebraska as eastern red cedar) berries. Each individual stakes out an area rich with juniper fruits and warbles out its territorial song, both to warn away other birds of the same sex and to attract a mate.

One of the few birds who sing territorial songs throughout the year, solitaires aggressively ward off competitors, including squirrels and other fruit-eating songbirds. I once saw a flock of two hundred Bohemian waxwings descend on a solitaire's prime juniper and set about consuming all the fruits, actually forming juniper berry brigades to pass the purple-red fruits from beak to beak.

The solitaire went ballistic, screaming, singing, fluttering his wings, swooping, and diving. I sympathized with him, imagining how I would feel if a group of strangers entered my kitchen and set about consuming everything in the pantry. But the solitaire singing in the distance this morning seems relatively serene as he perches on the tip of one of the junipers and warbles away.

Both crossbills and solitaires seem to be doing well in North America, where a substantial portion of our conifer forests are still intact and maturing, not to mention all the conifers invading our grasslands. Ornithologists estimate that more than ten million crossbills and one million solitaires occupy our forests and woodlands. And here they are, happily setting up shop at my prairie hideaway.

But what I've really come looking for on this cool June morning are the grassland birds, individuals who depend on healthy, intact prairies to survive. Once I leave the woodland behind, I begin to hear western meadowlarks warbling out their melodious cadenzas while perched atop shrubs and fence posts. The scattered singers raise their beaks to the sky, their lemon-yellow breasts gleaming in the sunlight.

Farther out, on a fencepost near the top of a dune, a graceful upland sandpiper stands on spindly legs surveying his surroundings through black, placid eyes. At intervals the perching sandpiper ruffles his feathers and lets out a liquid, wailing cry, a rolling "pulip, pulip, pulip."

This stirring call sends ripples through the flesh, evoking the wild beauty of the grass-covered dunes and the wonder of this upland shorebird's six-thousand-mile migration from the pampas of Argentina and Chile to the prairies of North America. Hearing this cry high overhead in Argentina in April, seventeenth-century explorer William Henry Hudson penned one of the most lyrical descriptions of bird migration ever created:

> Lying awake in bed, I would listen by the hour to that sound coming to me from the sky, mellowed and made beautiful by distance and the profound silence of the moonlit world, until it acquired a fascination for me above all sounds on Earth. . . .
>
> It was this sense of mystery it conveyed which so attracted and impressed me—the mystery of that delicate, frail, beautiful being,

SHOREBIRDS IN THE GRASS

traveling in the sky alone, day and night, crying aloud at intervals as if moved by some powerful emotion, beating the air with its wings, its beak pointing like the needle of a compass to the north, flying, speeding on its several-thousand-mile flight to its nesting home in another hemisphere.

"Elegant" is the operative word for upland sandpipers. Standing twelve inches tall with long, slender necks; small oblong heads; liquid black eyes; and two-inch-long, needle-straight beaks, these agile flyers glide over upland meadows, issuing their soul-stirring calls at regular intervals. While threatened in other areas of the Great Plains, upland sandpipers seem to be holding their own in the Sandhills, where they often perch on roadside fence posts.

I once made the mistake of stopping my car to photograph a female perched on one of these posts, quietly surveying her surroundings. It was the first week in June, when the young had just hatched, and I should have known better. With squeals and screams, she launched into the air, fluttered in place, then flew halfway into the open window, hovering within inches of my face.

Not just elegant but courageous as well. And to think that the male upland sandpiper I'm watching now has recently completed his solo journey without benefit of a map or compass, returning to the grassland of his birth. Recent research indicates they use the stars, the sun's position in the sky during various times of the day, and an internal magnetic compass to pull off this feat. But to do it alone, that's what impresses me the most.

So I give him a wide berth, angling back toward the ponderosas on my right and dropping down into a depression filled with knee-high clumps of green needle-and-thread grass and russet-red little bluestem.

After a minute or so, I hear a liquid, undulating "curle-e-u-u, curle-e-u-u" emanating from a ridgetop to my left and see the tawny-feathered crier lift off, circle, and flap toward me. The wailing cries amplify as the big shorebird zooms low across the grass, homing in on my head.

With a *whoosh*, the curlew banks and swishes by, crying out frantically. Then here comes a second one following the same flight path and issuing the same urgent cries before veering off at the last second. I back away and find a shady spot under a lone ponderosa at the edge of the woodland as the curlew pair scream their way back toward the ridgetop.

Studies indicate that curlews performing distraction displays typically fly off from their young indirectly, forming an obtuse angle between the approaching predator, the nest site, and themselves. Coyotes and some other predators may assume that the parents are flying directly away from the nest and search accordingly.

As the curlews flutter back toward the ridgetop directly to my west, I make a rough calculation and search the grassy depression off to the left with my binoculars. It takes only a few seconds to see a hint of movement, then to spy two fluffy, blonde-feathered young creeping in and out of the clumps of grass.

That's more than I need to see, and I get up and slink back into the woods. Predators typically kill more than half of curlew young within a few weeks after they hatch, and there's no need to attract attention to these helpless youngsters.

It's both exciting and poignant watching these largest of North American shorebirds defend their vulnerable grassland nests. Long-billed curlews breed in mixed-grass and shortgrass prairies throughout the western plains, northern Great Basin, and intermountain valleys of the Cascades and northern Rockies. They winter along coastlines from California and Virginia south to Costa Rica.

Fortunately for long-billed curlews, they never have to fly over vast expanses of ocean, as some curlew species do, but their migration route remains a mystery. In early spring, people walking at night along the beaches of Southern California report hearing their plaintive cries high overhead.

In coastal areas curlews use their nine-inch-long, downcurved bills to extricate crabs and shrimp from burrows in beaches and mud flats. In grassland nesting areas, they probe for invertebrates in wetlands while also nabbing large insects from patches of bare ground and tufts of grass. Families sometimes feed cooperatively, corralling grasshoppers one by one.

Once curlews arrive on their grassland nesting grounds, pairs face the daunting task of defending ground nests and young from a phalanx of predators, including eagles, hawks, magpies, coyotes, raccoons, weasels, badgers, and bull snakes. To accomplish this, they've developed an array of defensive behaviors, including plaintive cries, strafing, "crouch-running," concealment in the grass, and aggressive raising of wings and puffing up of feathers.

Curlews are cagey about establishing nest sites, with the male scraping out several shallow depressions in the sand before the female finally begins bringing grass and small sticks to the one she prefers. When incubating, females will hunker down so low and remain so still that a coyote can stroll within a few feet without seeing them. Early twentieth century researchers reported being able to walk right up to a nest and gently lift the female off her eggs.

Chicks start cheeping to their parents at least two days before their beaks break through the egg shell. They leave the nest within twenty-four hours of hatching, and their plaintive cheeps intermingle with the soft "wheets" and "curlees" of their parents as the family meanders through the grass. Females generally leave their young after two to three weeks, and males a week or two later.

At around thirty days of age, the young are entirely on their own. Of the four hatchlings in a typical nest, it's a minor miracle if one or two make it through midsummer to migrate independently to coastal wintering areas.

While always courageous and resourceful when it came to evading predators, curlews had little defense against market hunting, farms, and encroaching trees. Considered fairly common in the Upper Midwest during the mid-nineteenth century, they vanished entirely from Illinois by 1873 and from Minnesota by 1897. On the Great Plains, breeding habitat has been fractured by oil and gas exploration, replacement of native grasslands with GMO corn and soybeans, and invasion of deciduous trees, which provide perches for owls and hawks.

In the Intermountain West, poaching of nesting curlews remains a major concern. Of sixteen birds fitted with transmitters in southwestern Idaho in 2013, seven were eventually killed by presumed target shooters. Numbers of nesting pairs have declined by as much as 90 percent in some southwestern Idaho study areas.

According to North American Breeding Bird Survey data, fewer than 150,000 long-billed curlews likely remain in the United States and Canada. In the Sandhills, preservation of wetlands, along with rotational grazing practices that maintain diverse nesting and foraging habitats, may have stabilized nesting populations for now. But in other areas of the High Plains, native shortgrass and mixed-grass prairies are disappearing at an alarming rate.

Sadly, most other curlew species are declining in number as nesting habitat diminishes, and several are listed as endangered. Slender-billed curlews, which nest in peat bogs in the Siberian taiga, haven't been seen since 2007. The far eastern curlew, of marshes and lakeshores of northeastern Asia, is down to around thirty thousand individuals.

Eskimo curlews nested by the millions in the Arctic tundra of Alaska and Canada before market hunters began to find them. Hunters shot up to two million per year during the late 1800s. Grasslands that served as migratory and wintering habitat were plowed under, driving a critical food source, the Rocky Mountain grasshopper, to extinction. Eskimo curlews vanished within a few decades. They're now listed as "critically endangered," though not one has been documented or photographed for nearly sixty years.

While European American market hunters were killing off millions of Eskimo and long-billed curlews during the eighteenth and nineteenth centuries, writers throughout the British Isles celebrated the courage and beauty of their revered Eurasian curlew.

Eighteenth-century Scottish poet Robert Burns exulted, "I never heard the loud, solitary whistle of the curlew in a summer noon . . . without feeling an elevation of soul like the enthusiasm of devotion or poetry."

Noting the continued decline of curlew populations throughout Great Britain, contemporary English essayist Michael McCarthy wrote simply, "If we lose the curlew, we lose the sound of the British wilderness."

The same could be said for the Sandhills. More than any other sound, the cry of the curlew—born of the wind and surf and nostalgia for lost places—evokes the lingering elements of wildness in this pastoral landscape. Lying alone in my tent after sunset, I hear the curlews wailing in the grassy dunes just beyond the pines and feel a glimmer of hope for our ravaged Earth.

Swan Lake

After seeing the pair of trumpeter swans flying out from the marsh at the south end of the lake in March, I wondered where they might be nesting. Pine Lake seems to have a little too much boat traffic during late spring and summer to suit these elegant but reclusive nesters, by far the largest and most conspicuous water birds in North America.

I'd seen a few trumpeter swan families on various lakes throughout the Sandhills but never made a concerted effort to discover nesting sites. Then one evening, while browsing through the *Nebraska Atlas and Gazetteer*, I found four bodies of water in the western Sandhills called "Swan Lake."

Knowing that these lakes had been named during the 1880s, when homesteaders and ranchers first settled the region, and knowing that the swans had been wiped out from the Great Plains by 1900, I grew curious about the fate of the swans and whether any had returned to their namesake lakes. So, in early June I left my campsite at Pine Lake and set out to visit a couple of these remote bodies of water.

The one-lane asphalt road leading north toward Arthur County's Swan Lake twisted and tumbled through a sea of sun-washed dunes and improbably green valleys. After a wet spring in the Sandhills, the roadside ponds and marshes resonated with the whir of duck wings, the eerie "winnowing" sounds made as the wind rushed through the tails of diving snipes, and the rasping calls of nesting yellow-headed blackbirds.

When I stopped by a roadside wetland and listened, I could hear the frog-like "oonk-a-lunk" of an American bittern and the sweet "wichity-wichity-wichity" song of a common yellowthroat in the greening cattails. Russet-faced Wilson's phalaropes spun like tops in a shallow area, corralling invertebrates and other delicacies, while a graceful Swainson's hawk circled overhead.

After cresting Baldy Hill, a high point in Arthur County, the road glided down to Swan Lake, an expanse of sky-blue water encircled by grassy hills. Steep, shadowy dunes rose up on the far side.

I parked on a low hill along the eastern shore and scanned the water with binoculars. Almost instantly I saw a pair of magnificent white trumpeter swans, their breast and neck feathers tinted orange from minerals in their summer diets. They cruised effortlessly through a shallow area of sedges and bulrushes before emerging onto the open water. A tiny white cygnet paddled between them.

I didn't know whether to jump for joy or weep from relief and remorse. What we did to these graceful creatures seems unforgivable; their recovery, both miraculous and heroic.

During the drought years of the 1890s, some Sandhills residents killed trumpeter swans to ward off starvation. Caroline Sandoz Pifer, younger sister of celebrated writer Mari Sandoz and an ardent conservationist, once told me that folks shot both swans and curlews.

But it was the market hunters who ravaged the population. They killed the swans for their white feathers, used to adorn women's hats; their soft skins, used to make powder puffs; their meat; and even their eggs. By the early 1900s several scientists speculated that the species had been driven to extinction.

In 1917 naturalist Edward Howe Forbush wrote despairingly of their presumed loss: "In the glowing firmament rode the long "baseless triangles" of the Swans, sweeping across the upper air in exalted and unswerving flight, spanning a continent with the speed of the wind, their forms glistening like silver in the sunset glow. They presented the most impressive spectacle of bird life ever seen in North America."

Every once in a while we get lucky and are given a second chance to do the right thing. During the summer of 1919, a group of outdoor enthusiasts exploring a remote area of southwestern Montana known as Red Rocks Lakes spied a dozen or so enormous white birds in the distance. When they moved in for a closer look, they identified the birds as trumpeter swans, the first reported in North America for two decades.

By 1930 this isolated population had grown to around seventy individuals. Over the next several decades, biologists introduced some of these swans' offspring into lakes and marshes on the northern Great Plains, including Lacreek National Wildlife Refuge in southwestern South Dakota. By the 1970s breeding pairs had begun to make their way back to western Nebraska.

Something very special must have lured them back to the Sandhills. Over the phone, Nebraska Game and Parks Waterfowl Program manager Mark Vrtiska told me that trumpeter swans gravitate toward lakes with shallows chock-full of nutritious aquatic plants, muskrat huts where pairs place their nests, and expanses of open water.

Weighing as much as thirty pounds, trumpeters require up to one hundred yards to lift off from the water, using their big webbed feet like paddles to push them skyward. While the adults can usually ward off predators, cygnets are vulnerable, and only one or two in five survive to adulthood.

"Once the cygnets hit the water, they're pretty small, and anything from northern pike, raptors, and thunderstorms can get them," Vrtiska said.

High water quality seems essential to trumpeter swan reproductive success. Lakes in the Sandhills where bottom-feeding Asian carp have proliferated lose native vegetation and water clarity, and the swans avoid them. Warming global temperatures may contribute to the degradation of potential nesting lakes. As water temperatures go up, lake surface areas decrease, and nonnative vegetation may spread.

Still, trumpeter swan numbers in western Nebraska have gradually increased, to more than one thousand individuals today. Three decades after the discovery of the small remnant population at Red Rock Lakes, biologists found another, larger, remnant population in Alaska, providing a second source of eggs and cygnets to reintroduce into the swans' historic breeding range. With nesting populations reestablished in the upper Midwest, Northern Rockies, and the Pacific Northwest, the total North American population has grown to more than sixty-three thousand birds.

While walking along the shoulder of the deserted road, I watched the trumpeter swan family cruise back into the marsh and disappear among the cattails. With my spotting scope, I scanned the shore of the mile-wide lake. Way across on the other side, I could just make out the sparkling white shapes of another trumpeter swan pair and their three cygnets, among a green swath of cattails and bulrushes.

After a half hour or so, a rusty white pickup pulled up, and the young woman behind the wheel asked if I was okay. I told her about the swans.

"Aren't they beautiful," she said, beaming, before rattling on down the road.

Two young cowboys wearing big black Stetsons and sporting handlebar mustaches stopped and asked me the same question, which I was beginning to understand really means, "What on earth are you doing out here?"

"I'm watching the swans," I told them. "It's wonderful how you've protected these wetlands and allowed these beautiful birds to return on their own."

"Don't know that we had much to do with that," the driver responded, "but we'll take it."

Everyone I talked to along the road seemed perfectly content to see the swans, but no one expressed surprise or wonder at the sight of these seemingly exotic birds cruising across one of their lakes. Sandhills residents interact regularly with charismatic wildlife, including bald eagles, mink, river otters, and pronghorns. Maybe trumpeter swans are just a routine element of the daily landscape.

Pulling away from the lake, I continued up the road. A few miles north, I spied a pair of gleaming white trumpeters cruising across a farm pond with four fluffy young tucked between them. I sat in the car and watched as the adults slipped their long necks into the water, emerged masticating what appeared to be pondweed, and then dropped bits of it onto the surface. The cygnets bobbed up and down like corks as they dog-paddled feverishly from one morsel to another.

A few miles farther along, I found another family of six cruising through an immense cattail marsh extending more than a mile between two steep linear ridges of consolidated dunes. A white-tailed doe stood motionless in the glowing meadow in front of the swans, holding one foreleg poised in the air as she kept an eye on me.

After reaching State Highway 2, I cruised east to Seneca, then followed another twisting country road north toward Brownlee. Cherry County's Swan Lake nestles among a sea of heaving hills a few miles south of the North Loup River.

I came to an abrupt halt near the top of one of these dunes, where a twenty-inch-long female snapping turtle dripping with green algae had parked in the roadway, her speckled, yellow-brown eyes gleaming menacingly in the setting sun. I watched her amble into a roadside patch of sand, where she would likely dig a hole and deposit her eggs.

Then I slithered under a barbed-wire fence, climbed to the dune crest, and set up my spotting scope. Far across the lake, two pairs of white trumpeters escorted at least five miniscule young through the shallows.

After visiting three of the four Swan Lakes and eventually finding five pairs of nesting trumpeters, I asked Mark Vrtiska why the swans appear to be doing so well in the Sandhills.

"I think the big take-home message is that we reintroduced them into high-quality habitat. So if you're trying to recover any species, it comes back to being able to provide habitat and securing that habitat."

In these cynical times when anti-environmental activists question the value of the Endangered Species Act because we've fully recovered only a small percentage of listed species, the heartwarming resurgence of trumpeter swans offers a valuable lesson. First you stop whatever it is that's driving the species toward extinction—in this case market hunting. Then you make sure that adequate habitat remains protected. Period.

The problem is, there's always some economic interest that wants to take just a little more of that habitat, piece by piece. Invasive, human-adapted species creep in from the edges, and before you know it, populations of your protected species have dwindled to unsustainable numbers.

In the case of the swans, their own adaptability and resilience played a major role in their eventual salvation. Recently, they started foraging in cornfields in winter, and some families are pioneering new wintering sites in tiny streams, such as Blue Creek and Pine Creek, which are barely wider than the swans' bodies.

That might explain the pair I saw in March at Pine Lake, who must have been wintering in the upper Pine Creek inlet, where the creek runs only three feet wide. But the creek is spring fed, flows at an even rate year-round, and supports lots of aquatic vegetation, so the swans must find all they need there.

The largest numbers of Sandhills trumpeters overwinter on the Snake and Loup Rivers, which also remain ice free throughout the coldest months. Others overwinter on the Niobrara River and the North Platte.

What a life, living on remote lakes throughout the breeding season and then hopping over to spring-fed streams to overwinter. Not coincidentally, flowing hot springs in the Red Rocks Lakes area of Montana were what saved the Rocky Mountain population during the first two decades of the twentieth century. These hot springs kept some remote mountain streams, including Yellowstone's famed Firehole River, ice-free, allowing the swans to live in the region year-round and not have to risk being shot during migration.

Living in the same locations throughout most of their lives, trumpeter swans develop an intimate sense of place and belonging. They also forge close family ties. Adults often mate for life, and family groups travel together throughout most of the year, with the young typically staying with their parents until they reach breeding age at two or three.

During my second visit to Arthur County's Swan Lake in August, I watched the adult pair nearest to the road tenderly escorting their now silvery, half-grown cygnet across the open water and shallow marshes near the eastern shore. At intervals, the swans dipped their long necks into the water or turned "bottoms-up" to probe deeper into the muck.

I never saw the cygnet stray more than a few feet from its parents, and when it drifted off, one of them invariably swam over and coaxed it back. The swans seemed to be getting used to me, and now I could sit on a low hill overlooking the lake and watch them without feeling like a threatening interloper.

When I was away, their blaring, rhythmic calls began to echo through my dreams, and I found it hard to avoid cruising up to Swan Lake to visit them whenever I could get free. As summer turned toward fall, I wondered where exactly they would go when the lake froze over and how they would survive the coming winter.

During the last days of October, as the seasonal darkness began to close in, I couldn't resist checking up on the Arthur County Swan Lake pair one last time. When I arrived at the lake an hour before sunset, I could see the swan family huddled atop a muskrat house near the eastern shore. Then I noticed five more white specks out in the marsh. In the spotting scope, each one resolved as a trumpeter swan. Apparently all of the second family I'd seen far across the lake in June had made it through the summer.

Tens of thousands of geese, ducks, and coots honked and quacked out on the water, and every few minutes the trumpeters chimed in, their calls sounding like exuberant French horns. A bald eagle swooped low over the water, scattering the coots across the placid surface.

Then I heard the rippling, tremulous calls of sandhill cranes—great, ragged flocks of them floating southward over the lake as the sky turned crimson. I stood on a grassy knoll beside the roadway, captivated by the abundance of life and the gentle hum of the glowing landscape.

I remembered my Celtic ancestors' stories about mute swans mesmerizing travelers who visited sacred springs and luring them into the dark underworld. I realized that the trumpeters at Swan Lake had cast a similar spell on me, and that I would follow them almost anywhere.

The solitude was shattered by a siren, and here came a hay truck bumping along the two-track road circling the north end of lake. Every few minutes the truck stopped, its siren went off, and groups of bellowing Angus cattle responded by gathering around the vehicle to receive their evening rations. Eventually, the truck made a right turn onto the road and pulled up beside me.

"Pretty sunset," said the ranch owner.

"Among the best I've seen," I replied, "and all the cranes, and swans, and ducks, and coots . . . You live in a very beautiful place."

He told me he'd seen trumpeters nesting on the lake during each of the twenty years his family has lived there, and that one November he counted forty swans out on the water; and one early March, just as the ice was breaking up, more than fifty.

"Maybe it's the deeper water here, or maybe they're finding more to eat."

I expressed my admiration for the conservation contributions of the local ranching community, all they've done to make this scene possible.

"I don't know about that," he said. "But it's sure been a good year for the grass."

The next morning at dawn I could barely make out the silhouettes of all the waterfowl as the lake surface glimmered in soft indigo light. But I could hear them, and their honks, quacks, grunts, splashes, and wails rose to a crescendo as the eastern sky blazed fiery red.

Amid the clamor, I heard a series of brassy "ko-honk, ko-honks" off to my left and looked up just as the family of three swans circled low over the southeast shore and headed straight toward me. The two adults and their full-grown cygnet flew twenty feet over my head, trumpeting away, then dipped their wings before rerouting toward the rising sun.

Perhaps they were heading out to explore wintering areas along the Dismal River fifteen miles to the northeast, or maybe they were simply cruising over to a nearby lake to forage. I could only guess. But I was pretty sure that come next spring, they'd be back at Swan Lake, and so would I.

Black Cherry Moon

During the Black Cherry Moon, a most sacred time of the year, Plains Indian women and children would wander from one prairie ravine to another gathering chokecherries. They'd crush the ripe fruits and mix them with dried bison meat and bison fat to create pemmican, a winter staple.

They'd make a refreshing punch out of chokecherries mixed with water and set aside some of the fruits for use in ceremonies honoring a young woman's first menstruation. They'd dry the fruits in the sun, store them in fawn-skin bags, and add them to winter stews.

So central are chokecherries to Plains Indian economy and religion that the Black Cherry Moon, the full moon rising in late summer when chokecherries have ripened, signals the time when many tribes hold the annual sun dance.

This rite occurs on the full moon because, as Lakota shaman Black Elk explained in *The Sacred Pipe*, "The growing and dying of the moon reminds us of our ignorance which comes and goes; but when the moon is full it is as if the eternal light of the Great Spirit were upon the whole world."

To prepare for the ceremony, chosen men gather together a variety of sacred items, including a necklace of otter skin with several inscribed circles. The first circle is inscribed with a cross, with eagle feathers representing the four powers of the universe, hanging from the corners of the cross. Tied to the center of the circle is a plume taken from the breast of the eagle, the place nearest to the heart and center of the sacred bird and a gift to *Wakan-Tanka*, "who dwells at the depths of the heavens, and who is the center of all things."

They carve eagle-bone whistles, which make the sound of the golden eagle's voice, which is also the voice of *Wakan-Tanka*. They create rawhide images of the crescent moon, which represents the waxing and waning, living and dying of all things; the bright red sun, with a round circle of blue in the middle to represent the Grandfather and Creator; and a solid red circle to represent sacred Earth.

After smoking the sacred pipe and assembling the sacred items, several men go out to locate the perfect cottonwood to place at the center of the sun dance lodge. It was the cottonwood, said Black Elk, who taught the people how to build tipis (as children played with the folded leaves). Breaking off a small upper twig of this tree reveals a perfect five-pointed star within, a sign of the presence of the Great Spirit. And the rustling voice of the cottonwood leaves sends a prayer to the heavens.

Black Elk said that the person selected to cut down the chosen tree speaks these words: "Of all the many standing peoples, you, O rustling cottonwood have been chosen in a sacred manner. . . . You are a kind and a good-looking tree; upon you the winged peoples have raised their families; from the tip of your lofty branches down to your roots, the winged and four-legged peoples have made their homes. When you stand at the center of the sacred hoop you will be the people, and you will be as the pipe, stretching from heaven to earth."

What deep expression of our bonds with nature and reverence for all living things—emotions often repressed by European American culture. At the root of these rituals is the idea that everything is sacred, from a rock, to a blade of grass, to a rustling cottonwood, to a soaring eagle. Just imagine walking through a world where everything you saw, touched, or smelled felt sacred.

On the day of the full Black Cherry Moon, I rise well before sunrise, planning to walk slowly around the lake while savoring each breath and sensation.

The morning air feels crisp and radiant, as twisted branches of big cottonwoods along the lakeshore frame the misty lake surface and fiery sky. Concentric circles of knee-high sand muhly grass glow rose-red where the first sunlight touches the dunes. Off in the distance, the white-tailed doe and her spotted fawn pose on a sun-washed dune top, quietly watching.

Climbing the sandy ridge just south of the camping area, I brush through a patch of brilliant yellow sunflowers growing nearly head high. Every third or fourth flowerhead shelters a sleeping moth caterpillar—a lemon-yellow one curled around the brown disk of one flower, a big fat jade-green one curled up head to tail, and several smaller yellow-and-black caterpillars with dark bristles and sharp black spikes on their backs.

As I slosh my way down through the dew-covered grasses on the far side of the ridge, I notice a dozen or more three-inch-wide oblong objects glowing silver in the sunlight. Closer inspection reveals the shimmering, dew-coated wings of dragonflies clinging to the russet, bur-like fruits of wild licorice plants.

I place my index finger under one of the sleeping beauties, a maroon-bodied, white-faced meadowhawk. His tarsi prickle my warm skin while I hold him up for closer inspection.

Thousands of sparkling droplets of dew cover his thorax, the bristles on the back of his neck, his dark, sawtooth-edged legs—even the rims of his giant, maroon eyes. He holds on so tight that I have to brush his tarsi several times against the wild licorice burs before he will let go. But once settled, he seems to cling to his licorice-fruit bed just as complacently as he had before.

Larger, globular dewdrops sparkle in the sunlight on the stems of surrounding grasses. Close-up, each drop appears as a shimmering crystal ball displaying three-dimensional images of the grasses, pines, and sky.

Another cluster of the licorice fruits shelters a sleeping emerald-green sweat bee. His iridescent green head, thorax, and turquoise-striped abdomen, tucked in among a half dozen russet-red licorice burs, creates a glowing, pastoral image, too beautiful to exist by accident. A tiny dewdrop balances atop each of the thousands of hairs on his body.

Apparently some bees grow as many hairs as squirrels do, with each hair capable of holding uncountable grains of pollen. I gaze into his slate-colored, almond-shaped compound eyes—each filling half the profile of his head—and wonder what he might be thinking.

Unlike European honey bees and bumblebees, sweat bees tend to lead solitary lives, often tunneling into the ground or into rotting wood to nest. These tiny bees sometimes gravitate toward the salts in human perspiration; in Brazil and other areas of the tropics, sweat bees readily fly into human ears to lap up our sweat and earwax. Fortunately, none of the several dozen species recorded on the western plains appears to engage in this behavior. This individual seems as peaceful and harmless as could be, snuggled up in his wild licorice bed.

Closer to shore a dazzling male saddlebags dragonfly—so named because of the distinctive shape of the black markings at the base of his hind wings—clings to a glowing switchgrass stalk. The silvery light illuminating his transparent wings reveals dozens of riverlike veins framing at least a thousand rectangular and pentagonal cells, each glistening with multiple dewdrops. Not a bad solar array, a useful tool for a cool-blooded creature on a cool morning.

A few feet away, a male widow skimmer dragonfly clings to another cluster of licorice burs. His powder-blue wingtips and white inner wings dazzle in the sunlight, contrasting with his jet-black head and thorax.

Whenever I see dragonflies warming their wings in the morning light, I wonder how anything so exquisite could be condemned to such a short life. Most adults survive for only a few months. Could it be that those few months of life are as chock-full of insight and experience as our seventy years? Does the beauty they display radiate across the universe, enriching the lives of other species?

Of course, dragonfly lives are imbued with more than physical beauty. To other, smaller insects, these agile, fearsome-looking predators must cause continual panic and fear. Later in the morning, after they have become active, a significant number of the perched dragonflies I discover are munching away on a beetle, fly, or damselfly.

Through three hundred million years of evolution, dragonflies and damselflies have developed unique abilities to maneuver and accelerate in midair. Dragonflies can hover for several seconds, then dart forward or sideways at speeds approaching thirty-five miles per hour. Unlike birds and butterflies, they can rotate and flap each of their four wings independently, increasing their maneuverability and producing plenty of lift with less effort.

Dragonflies can even mate on the wing, and I've seen couples interlocked in "mating wheels" gliding through the cattails—with the male grabbing the female behind her head with the cerci on the tip of his tail while she curls her tail up to collect sperm from his abdomen.

Close-up, the heads of these winged jewels resemble something from a science fiction horror movie. Giant oval eyes and giant toothed mandibles dominate the face. Each of the two large eyes contains around thirty thousand facets, miniscule hexagonal lenses that all work together to create a three-dimensional image. But that's not all; dragonflies also have three "third eyes" embedded within a turret-like structure at the top of their head that help them detect light and movement.

The long, usually black legs sport hooked feet, perfect for gripping and squeezing. While watching a gorgeous male widow skimmer dragonfly munching away on a pale-blue forktail damselfly, I wonder how we can ever reconcile all the exquisite beauty that surrounds us with the constant pain and terror inherent in the natural world. British ethologist Richard Dawkins said that one of the hardest lessons humans have to learn is that nature is neither cruel nor pitiless.

"We cannot admit that things might be neither good nor evil, neither cruel nor kind, but simply callous."

It's a challenge trying to reconcile this awareness with a quote from Black Elk that I carry with me wherever I go: "Earth is your Grandmother and your Mother and she is sacred. Every step that is taken upon her should be as a prayer."

Perhaps honoring and accepting are the best we can do. And when I see a powder-blue dragonfly glistening in the morning light, I can't help feeling inspired by its beauty.

Down along the shore, a clump of gooseberry bushes sprouts up from the grassy embankment, and I pause to pick a dozen of their purple fruits. In the shallows nearby, white, three-petaled flowers of arrowhead root, also known as duck potato, sway in the morning breeze. I take out my pocket knife and cut off a few of the iris-like plants just below the surface, planning to throw the succulent tubers and stalks into the evening's supper pot.

I swish my way up through patches of switchgrass and prairie sandreed until I feel the ponderosa pine shadows reaching out. Beyond the pines, ankle-high sand cherry bushes blanket the dunes. In late June, while walking through this same area, I'd seen thousands of small green sand cherries on these plants. This morning, there's nothing but dirty-green leaves and dark stems.

After searching from one dune crest to another, my sand cherry harvest consists of two wilted red berries. That's it. The deer, voles, mice, raccoons, wild turkeys, lark sparrows, and other critters have gotten all the rest.

Peering out over the seemingly fruitless hills, I think of all I've been missing. The meadow voles scurrying through the tall grasses and sand cherries, sniffing, grooming, and courting in the moonlight. The little dung beetles rolling earth-shaped nurseries over the dunes. The badgers and weasels snuffling along, seeking out ground squirrels and kangaroo rats. The hiss of the grasses in the evening breeze as they suck up moisture from the dunes and reach for the stars.

It's as if I've been camped on the tip of an iceberg, with no awareness of the 90 percent below the surface. I take a second look around and become aware of the complex textures of the native grasses covering the dunes. Over to the right, a shady hollow cradles a dense patch of waist-high, burgundy-tinted little bluestem.

A close look at the stems of this delicate grass reveals some of the most striking wildflower blossoms imaginable. A dozen deep-maroon, bell-shaped stamens dangle on slender threads from individual spikes, while feathery-white, cone-shaped female parts nestle among them.

Nearby, stalks of chest-high switchgrass glow crimson in the morning light. Their flowers reveal themselves as glistening orange bells dangling below fuzzy magenta stigmas—the visible portion of the female parts, designed to catch pollen.

Higher up on the dune, the silvery, three-pronged seedheads of sand bluestem reveal blond stigmas bursting from flaxen seedheads. A few bronze stamens hang limp, having already released their pollen.

I've realized for a long time that grasses are, indeed, flowering plants, but most field guides don't show the flowers, and to see these vivid beauties close-up inspires awe and respect. Imagining the stamens bursting forth and releasing millions of grains of golden pollen while the fuzzy stigmas wait expectantly in the morning breeze compels me to embrace the grasses as sexual beings, just like us.

Viewed through the hand lens, the bell-shaped male parts appear vibrant and showy; the pine-cone-shaped stigmas, sticky and seductive. I can just make out a few tiny golden grains sprinkled over their surfaces. Upping the magnification to 20x, it becomes apparent that each of the hundreds of individual bristles on one rice-sized stigma branches out into an array of translucent subbranches, many of which hold a globular pollen grain.

Silvery sunlight flows through every part of this vermicelli-like web, fueling the complex transformation to follow. The minute pollen grain, stimulated by its contact with the sticky stigma, grows a pollen tube extending down through the pistil to the ovary, then releases sperm cells to float down and fuse with an unfertilized egg.

The male parts of grass flowers are designed to release as much pollen as possible, the female parts to stretch out and capture it as it streams by. The timing of this mutual unfurling seems synchronized throughout small patches of prairie, and I can't help wondering if the individual grasses are speaking to one another.

Recent studies have established that grasses send out chemicals described as "green leafy volatiles" (think of the aroma of recently mowed grass) to defend themselves from threats. When legions of voracious caterpillars descend on a single grass plant, the plant may emit a specific volatile that attracts parasitic wasps who then lay their eggs in the bodies of the caterpillars. Neighboring grass plants not yet invaded by the caterpillars sense this chemical release and send out wasp-attracting chemicals of their own.

Grasses must also communicate chemically through their networks of roots and tillers, and I can imagine that a sudden release of pollen by some grasses might fill the air and ground with aromas stimulating nearby plants to stretch out their panicles to catch the golden grains.

I can begin to visualize a communication network extending most of the way across North America. After all, the celebrated "tallgrasses," such as big bluestem, Indian grass, and switchgrass, thrive from Arizona to Maine. Their web of cooperative energy has evolved over at least fifty million years. My species is a very recent visitor to this enchanted world, and I feel honored to sit on this hillside watching the flowered grass stems dance in the morning breeze.

Field studies indicate that each grass plant pays close attention to the angle of the sun, the warmth of the air, and the strength of the breeze to determine when to open its stamens and release millions of grains of pollen. Under a strong wind, the grains may overshoot their target—conspecifics growing downwind—and sail for hundreds of miles. Botanists 625 miles out in the Atlantic have collected grass pollen from the Scottish Highlands.

But the cleverest tallgrasses typically release their pollen in midmorning, when breezes remain relatively light. The fuzzy female parts lie in wait, stretching their sticky stigmas in hopes of catching a few passing grains.

A study of meadow fescue grass in Norway concluded that most of the pollen captured by the stigmas originated within a few yards of them, and that taller plants captured more pollen than smaller plants. Meanwhile, active tillering just beneath the surface enables grasses to expand their footprint without having to rely on sexual reproduction.

Seed dispersal is another story. Grass seeds are relished by dozens of prairie bird species, and some may fly a half mile or more with the seeds in their beaks. If the grasses are designed to attract anything, it's probably avian seedeaters and grazing mammals. Do the grasses strategize? Are they aware of who is doing the munching and dispersing? Does herbivory hurt or tickle? We have so much to explore and learn.

And what a joy to find all these gorgeous native grasses thriving on these sand hills. All over the western prairies, native grasses are being supplanted by Eurasian imports, including smooth brome, cheatgrass, quackgrass, red top, timothy, and Canada bluegrass.

This supplanting of the natives contributes to a homogenization of the prairie that inhibits breeding opportunities for some small mammals and grassland-nesting birds. There's no longer enough diverse growth in many areas to provide them with sufficient foraging opportunities and enough protected niches in which to place their nests.

To experience a mostly native prairie like this one, feel the grasses swishing against the legs, and admire their inviting blossoms stimulates feelings of hope and renewal. We can save native species and native ecosystems if we're willing to adapt our land uses to their needs.

No one knows for sure why native grasses appear to do so much better in the Sandhills than in surrounding prairies, but certainly the predominant land use—cattle ranching—and the scarcity of humans (about one resident per square mile) have a lot to do with it. There just aren't as many roads, towns, farms, and feedlots fragmenting this prairie.

Less disturbance means more native grass cover and fewer opportunities for weeds to invade. It's also possible that the sandy soil is less hospitable to some of the most aggressive weeds, especially smooth brome and cheatgrass, fast-growing grasses imported from Eurasia that are rapidly taking over grasslands throughout western North America.

On properties surrounding this wildlife area, ranchers have used rotational grazing to stimulate grass growth. Cattle are moved from one pasture to another every few weeks, mimicking the actions of nomadic bison. The grasses respond to this intense, short-term grazing by sending out new roots and tillers, and the bovine fertilizer fuels renewed growth.

But this wildlife area hasn't been grazed for decades, and while some weedy species are visible nearly everywhere, the native grasses still appear to be thriving. I think the lightness of our footprint on this landscape has a lot to do with that.

On this sunny August morning, the curing grasses smell

delicious—musty, nutty, and sweet. I know that aroma deep down. It lured my most distant ancestors out of the forests and into the glowing savannas of tropical Africa. It enticed my Celtic ancestors westward across North America. It nourished the cattle, horses, and sharp-tailed grouse inhabiting the sand hills surrounding my great-great grandparents' sod house near Haigler, Nebraska.

The earthy smell of curing grass entranced me when my brothers and I would build sod forts behind our childhood home in Northern California. Grass flows through our blood, ingested as wheat, rice, oats, barley, corn—even sugarcane and bamboo shoots. It's as much a part of our being as air and water. A few moments curled up in a patch of pliant switchgrass or velvety Indian grass on a fresh August morning revive primal feelings of comfort and connection.

Native American cultures continue to speak of grass as a sacred partner. In *Braiding Sweetgrass*, botanist and gifted nature writer Robin Wall Kimmerer, a member of the Citizen Potawatomi Nation, describes the joy of holding a braided sweetgrass bundle up to your nose:

"Find the fragrance of honeyed vanilla or the scent of river water and black earth and you understand the scientific name: *Hierochloe odorata*, meaning the fragrant, holy grass. In our language it is called *wiingaashk*, the sweet-smelling hair of Mother Earth. Breathe it in and you start to remember things you didn't know you'd forgotten."

But somehow along the way, "grass as far as the eye can see" became an epithet instead of a revelation among European Americans. It might have been a matter of simple economics and survival. The exotic grasses from Eurasia and Mexico that homesteaders grew as crops, including Eurasian wheat and Central American corn, produced higher yields than the native grasses, so many people in subsequent generations discarded the natives from conscious thought. Now tourists drive across the grasslands without even seeing them, hurrying to the mountains. They have no idea what they're missing.

Energized by the textures and aromas of the sunlit grasses, I climb to the crest of the highest dune, which affords a panoramic view of the soft green hills across the lake. I reach down and break off a sprig of silver-gray pasture sage, crush it between my palms, and rub the pungent herb into my beard and hair.

Plains Indians burn pasture sage to purify sweat lodges and sanctify religious ceremonies. But it's also good for refreshing the spirit, pretending that you're mosquito proof, and celebrating small discoveries.

On the way back I stop by the lakeshore where a few head-high chokecherry shrubs huddle at the base of a steep dune. I find two dozen deep purple berries, but since this is the only chokecherry source around this side of the lake, I pick just four. Anyway, they remain intensely acerbic at this time of year (hence the European American name, "chokecherry") and won't become sweet when picked until after the first frost, when they shrivel up like raisins. And I have no plans to make pemmican.

Back at camp, after an afternoon of reading and napping in the shade, I heat up a small pot of vegetable stock and throw in the arrowhead roots, some cattail tubers, and a handful of leaves from the Rocky Mountain bee plant. I savor this earthy stew one small bite at a time, accompanied by fresh spearmint tea, saving the gooseberries, two sand cherries, and four chokecherries for dessert.

My mother, a creative and energetic cook, would have been appalled by this pathetic excuse for dinner. But maybe on some level she would have understood.

As the Black Cherry Moon eases up through the cottonwoods on the far shore and its golden light splashes across the lake surface, the owls begin to call, one by one.

"Who-whoo, whoo-whoo." Great horned owl.

"Whoot . . . whoot . . . whoot." Long-eared owl, way off in the shadowy pines.

Then a high, descending wail, like a whinnying horse. Eastern screech-owl.

Out on the water Canada geese, wood ducks, and western grebes honk, squeal, and flutter their wings. Overhead, a half dozen crows caw out warnings as they flap toward their roost in the pines.

All my relations.

Milkweed Silk

The silvery, iridescent sheen of milkweed silk dazzles the eyes and suggests a universe of miracles lurking within. Showy milkweed, the tallest of the three milkweed species at the lake, goes to seed in early fall. As its tan, horn-shaped fruit pods dry and split open, the contents burst into fist-sized, cottony clumps consisting of dozens of oblong seeds and thousands of attached threads.

Gleaming in the sunlight like miniature supernovas, these silk puffs splinter and fray in the wind until the seeds break loose and sail across the prairie. A close-up look at the seeds and their gossamer parachutes reveals an intricate and elegant architecture. Hundreds of inch-long threads attach to each black, oblong seed in a funnel array. Each hollow thread resembles a miniature cellophane noodle.

The threads twist and curl near their tips, forming a foil to catch the wind. If you hold a milkweed seed in your palm on a calm morning and set it adrift, the seed and attached silk float toward the ground in slow motion, like a jellyfish descending through still water.

Milkweed silk has entranced prairie dwellers for centuries. Cheyenne and Lakota children played with the seeds, casting them to the breezes and chasing them through the swaying grasses. This practice may have contributed to the tendency of milkweed plants to proliferate around Plains Indian villages—not a bad thing, since common, showy, and swamp milkweed, though containing powerful toxins, are edible during some stages of their growth, and their flowers rank among the most fragrant on the prairie.

European settlers used the downy milkweed silk to stuff their pillows and mattresses. In the 1860s a cottage industry developed in Salem, Massachusetts, around the creation of milkweed-stuffed pillows and comforters. During World War II the U.S. government encouraged scout groups and farmers to collect dried milkweed pods and ship them to central collecting stations. The hollow silk threads, many times more buoyant than cork, were stuffed into life jackets.

North American Indians used virtually every part of the milkweed plant, including the silk. In *The Herbal*, published in London in 1633, John Gerard wrote, "The silke [*sic*] is used of the people of Pomeiocand and other of the Provinces adjoyning, being parts of Virginia, to cover the secret parts of maidens." Other uses of the silk included swaddling for babies and insulation for buffalo robes.

During the late 1980s, a Nebraskan named Herb Knudson created the Ogallala Down Company. He had been doing research for Standard Oil Company on using the sticky white milkweed sap for fuel and milkweed silk for facial tissues. When these projects fizzled, he decided to put his knowledge about milkweed to direct use. Now, thousands of people around the world sleep under plush comforters filled with the same natural material that enveloped Lakota and Pawnee infants.

For many years my only relationship with milkweed silk was through the close-up lens of my camera. The wispy puffs, with their internal rainbows of refracted light, pulled me like gravity, until I wanted to lose myself in that silken universe and discover what lay within. But the focal length of the lens (about six inches) always stopped me short.

I finally decided that if I really wanted to gain intimate knowledge of the silk, I should set about becoming fully acquainted with the plant that produces it. So one year I devoted a good part of the growing season to observing milkweeds.

In late May I found the first green shoots of showy milkweed protruding from the muddy soil beneath last year's dried plants. They looked like naked asparagus stalks pushing up through bunches of nettle and fragrant spearmint, though some had already sprouted pairs of tiny oval leaves.

I cut three shoots off a few inches above the ground and threw them into a pot of boiling water. After a couple of minutes, I poured off the water, added some more, and repeated the process.

The idea is to reduce the toxicity of the plants. Although spring shoots are considered less toxic than the mature fruit pods, all parts of milkweed are poisonous. The toxins, which include cardiac glycosides, resinoids, and alkaloids, can cause stomachache, vomiting, or worse (including "coma," according to a USDA publication). These toxins are what make monarch caterpillars and butterflies distasteful to most birds, a sort of travel insurance policy that enables most adult monarchs emerging east of the Rockies in early fall to complete an annual migration to the mountains of Michoacán, in central Mexico.

Some folks eat the shoots raw, but since I was camping alone I decided to cook them first. The boiled shoots tasted like green beans, only slightly bitter, and I washed them down with fresh mint tea to dilute the effect.

Soon after, I began to feel a tingling sensation in my fingers. Probably hypochondria. Nevertheless, I left showy milkweed off the menu for the remainder of the trip.

By June the milkweed stalks had sprouted large oblong leaves with prominent white veins and ball-shaped clusters of star-shaped, pink-and-cream flowers. The flower clusters seemed so fragrant that savoring them felt slightly wicked, like engaging in illicit sex. Essence of Easter lily with a hint of jasmine and musk. It was tempting to sample every blossom, but there was stiff competition from an array of intoxicated native bees, bumblebees, and honeybees who buzzed around and within each cluster.

There was something about the lily-like aroma that filled me with twinges of longing and sweet sadness, and then I remembered. I was holding my mother's right hand, walking across a green cemetery lawn buzzing with honeybees. She clasped a bouquet of large white lilies wrapped in tissue paper in her left hand. We walked into a big rectangular marble building, cool inside and richly scented with fresh-cut lilies and roses. Our footsteps echoed off the polished walls.

My mother walked over to a workbench and picked up a metal tulip-stem vase and a long metal rod. She trimmed the flowers, placed them in the vase, added water from a rusty metal faucet protruding from the wall, then inserted the vase into a metal loop on the end of the rod. I felt a little scared, but I liked the coolness of the air, the sweet smells, and the hollow echoing of our footsteps on the smooth marble.

We walked over to the west wall, and she extended the rod high up, almost to the ceiling. The wall was covered with marble squares bearing the names of dead people. She carefully inserted the vase into a slot in front of one of the squares. The inscription read: "James L. Kelly, 1916–1942."

I'm sure my mother had told me that we were going to visit her brother's grave, but it didn't sink in until I saw her place the flowers high up on the wall. I wondered why anyone would want to be buried in a marble wall. I was smart enough not to ask that question.

Kay rarely spoke of her brother. A few years later I would grow to understand that he was her only sibling and was completing graduate work at Stanford University when he came down with Hodgkin's disease. He was one of my father's graduate student friends, and that's how my father, a native Nebraskan whose family had homesteaded on the western plains and opened clothing businesses in Lincoln during the 1880s, met my mother.

Later, I found my uncle Jim's picture in a box of family photos in the top shelf of my bedroom closet. He looked confident and sincere. I thought he looked a little like my grandfather and quite a bit like me.

I loved my grandparents and spent a part of each summer at their little red house on the farm, but they rarely spoke of their lost son. However, their early retirement was hastened by debilitating physical conditions that may or may not have been related to their grief. There was my grandfather's mysterious upper back condition, sometimes referred to as "arthritis," that left him crippled and in constant pain the last twenty years of his life. After several unsuccessful surgeries, he died addicted to opioids and barely coherent. And my grandmother's hospitalization for a "nervous breakdown" was followed by the loss of all her hair before she was sixty. My grandmother frequently told me she didn't believe in "living in the past," her only oblique reference to the loss of her son.

As children we barely sense the significance of family trage-
dies. As adults we struggle to understand how they help shape us
and send us careening toward unforeseen destinies. All I know is
that shortly before she died, my mother told me that her brother's
death was so painful that afterward she just didn't permit herself
to feel intense emotions. "I couldn't go through that again," she
said. And shortly after I turned seventeen, I developed an afflic-
tion eerily similar to the one that had crippled my grandfather.

So maybe those repressed family memories, triggered by my rec-
ollections of the aroma of the flowers in my uncle's resting place,
explain why the milkweed aroma mesmerizes me. Or maybe I'm
attracted to the flowers for the same reason that the bees are. I've
read that the bees share 80 percent of our genes, and I'd be willing to bet that among them is a "flower nectar attractant" gene,
or something of the sort.

Human olfactory abilities have become so eroded that we miss
out on some of nature's most intimate pathways. Imagine a salmon
smelling his way back to the tiny brook where he was born. Or a
leatherback turtle sniffing her way across thousands of miles of
ocean to her natal beach. Or a wolf sensing fresh blood three miles
away. I've read that a sheep in a flock of several hundred can find
her lamb by scent alone.

As humans, we rarely experience the intense, primordial power
of smell. It takes something as overpowering as a showy milkweed
flower to get our attention.

I set up my tripod and began to photograph the flower clusters
and insects close-up. One image captured a bright orange ladybug, an iridescent blue leafhopper, and a European honeybee, all
nestled into one fragrant cluster. Another revealed a pale-green
crab spider scurrying through a jungle of pink-white blossoms.
Her plump abdomen bore swatches of pink that matched the color
of the flower petals.

One honeybee stayed put as I homed all the way in with my
lens, until her image filled the frame. Her left hind leg dragged
behind, apparently trapped in a flower's center, and her whole
body vibrated as she struggled to break free. On the same flower

cluster, another honeybee sported tiny yellow pollen-bearing sacs on the end of each hind leg.

The bees, attracted by the flowers' rich colors and captivating aroma, get their hind legs caught in slender, sticky, threads called translators that fuse the flowers' pollen sacs together. Sometimes the bee loses a leg or remains ensnared and dies.

If the bee struggles loose, the pollen sacs, which resemble tiny saddlebags, remain attached to her hind legs, to be carried to another flower where they get inserted into a stigmatic slit that leads into the ovary. Somehow during the flight, the pollen sacs rotate ninety degrees, so when the bee arrives at the new flower, they are perfectly aligned to fit into the stigmatic slit.

This intimate and curious process, imbued with overtones of volition and guile, offers a hint of what can be accomplished in a couple of hundred million years. During that time, milkweeds evolved flowers like no others, and their unique flower structure ensures that pollen grains get carried away to other individual flowers, boosting genetic diversity.

Showy milkweed flowers look like inverted starfish. Actually, the starfish-like part we notice is a feature unique to milkweeds, called a corona. The actual petals and sepals are less noticeable, as they usually curve downward, away from this prominent feature. Within the corona, five pink, horn-shaped hoods (the "arms" of the starfish) reach outward and curve slightly upward.

Inside the hoods, the five stamens fuse to the cylindrical stigmatic surface, their pollen sacs joined together by the translators. The whole intricate, enticing structure seems deliberately designed to lure honeybees and make sure they don't get away without a leg full of pollen.

If intelligence is the ability of creatures to gauge their surroundings and evolve strategies for success, milkweeds must be about as clever as they come. I bent down and took a few more sniffs.

On one of the larger milkweed leaves, a whole herd of glowing yellow aphids grazed their way across the fuzzy surface. The aphids on the broad green leaf reminded me of bison out on the prairie, a pastoral family of herbivores dotting the nearly flat landscape.

These oleander aphids, sometimes called milkweed aphids,

are made to procreate. The all-female babies emerge with the next generation's fetus already inside them and can give birth within a week. In a predator-free world, a single aphid and subsequent generations could engender several trillion aphids in one season.

Like other insects that consume milkweed, the aphids have learned to control the flow of milkweed toxins into their bodies. They literally farm the milkweed leaves, pinching off the veins leading to the areas where they plan to graze.

Their Day-Glo color warns predators away, but fortunately for milkweeds and gardeners, many predatory insects have little trouble digesting these juicy aphids. So on every tenth milkweed plant, I found bright orange, white-spotted or black-spotted ladybugs, the wolves of this particular prairie ecosystem.

In addition to a half dozen species of ladybug, I discovered funnel-web spiders, daddy longlegs, soldier bugs, assassin beetles, long-horned beetles, and parasitic wasps that lay their eggs in the aphids' bodies.

The most seemingly fearsome insects were the green lacewing larvae, half-inch-long, yellow-and-brown crawlers that resemble elongated, soft-bodied sow bugs. They pierce the aphids' bodies with their sharp mandibles, sucking out the guts. My pastoral scene had grown edgy.

The following morning, I got up before sunrise and visited several flower clusters, scraping the dew off and depositing it in a small glass jar. I added a few, choice flower parts for extra flavor. I took the mixture back to camp, added a little water, and boiled it down until it turned viscous and brown.

In *Edible Wild Plants of the Prairie*, naturalist Kelly Kindscher writes that French Canadians used milkweed dew to sweeten their crêpes. Lakota women gathered the dew-covered flowers whole and pressed or boiled them. Since I'm not fond of pancakes, I poured the syrupy mixture onto my morning cereal and added some milk. The result was satisfying, faintly sweet and redolent of lily.

By early August the flowers had ripened into green, croissant-shaped pods with a warty surface. One morning a few years before, I had plucked a couple, thrown them into a pot, and brought them to a boil three times, changing the water after each boiling. The slippery concoction tasted like okra but without the crunch.

Plains Indians cooked up a stew of boiled milkweed pods and buffalo meat. Kindscher says that the Omahas and Pawnees, after seeing cabbage prepared by white explorers, called it "white man's milkweed." Kindscher subsisted partially on showy and common milkweed pods while trekking across Kansas and eastern Colorado for eighty days. He characterized these slimy delicacies as his "favorite wild foods from the prairie."

By late September, the milkweed pods at Pine Lake had turned tannish white and begun to split open, revealing tufts of cottony silk. Just after sunrise, in a shady hollow not far from camp, I came upon a red and black milkweed beetle sleeping within a shimmering ball of milkweed silk. The beetle nestled into a crevice where the horn-shaped pod had opened to extrude a ball of fluffy silk and seeds.

Each brown, oblong seed sported a cup-shaped array of more than one hundred silver threads, fully unfurled and ready to catch the first breeze. I homed in with the hand lens, hoping to finally discover what might lie inside the threads.

At first glance, they looked perfectly translucent. But under full magnification, some displayed grass-like textures and bamboo-like joints, along with pulses of rainbow light.

Something seemed to be floating around inside one of the silk threads. I imagined a one-celled creature unknowingly hitching a ride across the prairie, with a window seat all the way.

In a large milkweed patch nearby, I saw more discernible hints of activity. Before long, I was down on the ground photographing insects of every imaginable variety perching on, chewing on, crawling up, and hanging from the leaves and pods: ladybugs, dragonflies, grasshoppers, leaf hoppers, buffalo tree hoppers, bumblebees, funnel-web spiders, crab spiders, crane flies, lacewings, long-horned beetles, metallic flea beetles, milkweed bugs.

My favorites were the milkweed beetles, brilliant red with black spots and hundreds of frosty white hairs on their folded wings. The close-up lens revealed that their turquoise and black-striped antennae grow right through the middle of their black eyes, so that half of each eye can look down at their food and the other half can gaze upward for predators. Though with their intense warning color and their bodies chock-full of milkweed toxins, it didn't seem likely they had much to worry about.

A tiny snout bug crawled across a broad, concave leaf. At first glance the insect appeared drab brown, with its long snout pointing up toward the sky. Through the macro lens, its wings morphed into parchment scrolls ornamented with complex geometric patterns. A nearby pair of green and blue leafhoppers had the yellow letters "H" and "M" clearly inscribed on the back of their heads.

After a couple of hours of photographing various insects and looking under hundreds of leaves, I finally discovered what I had most wanted to see. Brilliant yellow, with black-and-white, horizontal stripes and horn-like antennae, the monarch caterpillar clung to the underside of a green-yellow leaf, calmly munching away at the ragged edge.

The caterpillar's pigments appeared so bright—a clear warning to potential predators—that I had trouble focusing the lens. I watched it for several minutes and noted its length—around two inches—a sure sign that it would pupate within a couple of days.

When I returned to the same plant the next morning, the caterpillar had vanished. I searched all the grasses and wildflowers within ten yards of the host plant, with no success. There had to be a chrysalis dangling from a leaf or stem somewhere. Monarch caterpillars invariably wander away from their host plants before pupating, seeking out an inconspicuous, sheltered spot to dangle for ten to twelve days.

My search efforts grew more and more frustrating. I had photographed a monarch chrysalis once before, in a terrarium, and I thought it was the most exquisite thing I'd ever seen—a jade-green teardrop with flecks and bands of gold. I wanted to photograph one in the wild and then return to photograph the emerging butterfly. But no luck. I would have to find more caterpillars, or stumble upon a chrysalis by chance.

After spending much of that morning turning over milkweed

leaves and slinking through the grass, I'd found two more cater-pillars but no chrysalises.

The following morning, my last at the lake, I was crunching my way through a frosty meadow close to shore when I spied a flash of orange down in the grass. This was not what I had been look-ing for but something equally compelling: an old, beat-up, frost-encrusted monarch clinging upside down to a bending stalk of goldenrod.

Her wings, cinnamon-orange with thick black veins, had been shredded to two-thirds of their normal size, possibly from wear and tear or encounters with birds. She appeared no more alive than the dry cottonwood leaves scattered around her.

I waited and watched. As the rising sun warmed the crystals of frost on her wings, they transformed into spherical droplets. After awhile the droplets sagged and began to dribble away, and the wings began to flex.

Clouds of spiraling mist rose off the lake, as the monarch's rag-ged wings stretched out to receive the sun's life-sustaining rays. After another thirty minutes, the monarch finally fluttered off toward the north, flailing across the grass toward a warmer perch in the surrounding dunes.

That was miracle enough. But later that morning, a new mon-arch came flying in from that same direction. This gorgeous, smoky-orange male also flew awkwardly, tilting and tossing in the light breeze, but he appeared noticeably larger and gleamed with freshness.

He alighted on a golden box elder bush a few feet from shore. The monarch dangled from a maple-like leaf, swiveling back and forth in the breeze. I could see remnants of his chrysalis dangling from his abdomen and guessed that this glowing, pristine butter-fly had emerged within the past couple of hours.

I watched and photographed him for several minutes, then walked back up the hill to brew a cup of coffee. When I returned a few minutes later, the monarch still clung to the underside of the leaf, his tawny wings aglow in the morning light.

I crouched in the grass beneath the box elder bush and raised my left hand toward the dangling butterfly. I could see his long black antennae testing the air and his coal-black eyes—little pin-heads embedded in a confusing array of white spots. When my index finger rubbed against the leaf, he jumped right on board.

His prickly black legs tickled my skin as he rested between my thumb and index finger, gently opening and closing his wings. I walked him over to a cottonwood stump and sat there facing the sun. The breeze strengthened and lifted him up like a sail, and his clasping tarsi tugged at my skin.

I, too, began to shiver a bit in the breeze. What was I thinking when I enticed this exquisite, delicate creature onto my warm hand? How would he survive this world of cold fronts, frosts, predators, pesticides, highways, and cities? How could he possibly fly all the way to central Mexico and partway back again?

Fifteen hundred miles is a long way for anyone to travel, but this gossamer-winged butterfly would attempt the journey without benefit of directions, guidance, or prior experience. Experiments suggest that monarchs use a "sun compass"—consisting of a matched awareness of the position of the sun in the sky and time of day—to navigate from the eastern and central United States to one of a handful of small monarch preserves clustered ten thousand feet up in the Sierra Madre Mountains of central Mexico. They may also use sensitivity to the earth's magnetic field to help them navigate on cloudy days.

With luck, this monarch would complete the journey in a couple of months and spend most of the winter dangling from an Oyamel fir within one of the preserves. Come spring, he would head north, in the general direction of western Nebraska, stopping a few hundred miles along the way to mate and die.

The next generation would continue the northward migration, then the next generation, until, come summer, direct descendants of the butterfly clinging to my hand would flit over the milkweeds and waving grasses of the western Sandhills.

But the "protected" montane forests in the monarch preserves are disappearing fast. The Mexican government has neither the resources nor the political clout to keep local villagers from cutting down the trees for firewood and clearing forests for agriculture.

Even more ominous, warming winters are allowing hordes of

beetles to infect the firs, killing thousands of trees. Unseasonably warm weather during winter stimulates sleeping butterflies to arouse and go looking for food. With no nectar available, they quickly burn off their remaining fat and die.

As warming progresses, it's possible that all the Oyamel firs will eventually die off, leaving the monarchs without winter shelter. Will they find another forest refuge in Mexico? It's doubtful, given the ongoing clear-cutting of remaining conifer forests.

Up here in the north, herbicides sprayed on and around fields of genetically modified crops have eliminated millions of acres of monarch habitat. Collisions with automobiles kill truckloads of monarchs each summer. Draining and destruction of wetlands have left billions of milkweed plants, the only host for the monarchs' eggs and larvae, high and dry.

And along the southward migration route, irrigated wheat and GMO corn crops are displacing native grasslands throughout vast areas of New Mexico, West Texas, and northern Mexico. Fall-migrating monarchs, who depend on nectar from native goldenrods and other sunflowers, are dropping dead from starvation long before they reach Michoacán.

During a recent winter, the number of monarchs wintering in the forests of Michoacán was 4 percent of historic averages. Average numbers from 2016 to 2020 were 20 percent of numbers recorded twenty years earlier.

In California, butterfly watchers have documented a more than 95 percent decline in numbers of monarchs overwintering in coastal sites. During a recent winter, several hundred volunteers monitoring monarch winter roosts along the California coast counted fewer than thirty thousand butterflies. Twenty years earlier, these same roosts supported more than a million butterflies. Some ecologists are predicting that monarchs may go extinct by the end of this century.

This possibility transcends feelings of loss and heartbreak. Sure, we've wiped out thousands of the world's animal species already and are well on our way to destroying most of the coral reefs and tropical rain forests, our most species-rich environments. But to eliminate monarch butterflies, one of the most elegant, revered, and resourceful creatures on earth, seems far beyond the pale.

I imagine a four-year-old child playing in a grassy meadow sweet with the aroma of milkweed flowers but with no monarch butterflies to play with. It seems to me that if we achieve this final sacrilege, we will have established once and for all that we simply don't belong here. The honorable thing to do would be to ride off into the sunset, leaving stewardship of this sacred planet to creatures far less destructive than us.

The miracle clinging to my hand seemed to hold, in one fragile package, all the beauty and divine aspirations of every creature that ever existed. I wondered whether this most recent intrusion—my sitting in the sun with the butterfly basking on the back of my hand—might somehow doom him to oblivion. What if I coughed or sneezed or absentmindedly brushed my right hand with my left? Then the breeze came up again, and his gossamer wings began to flutter.

After one last tug at my skin, he lifted off, flitting buoyantly to a bending willow a few yards away. I followed him over to a leafy branch where he basked in the sun, gathering his strength, plotting his course. A few minutes later he fluttered skyward and wafted south over the dunes.

By the time he crossed the border somewhere between Nogales and Ciudad Juarez, the first autumn cold fronts would have swept down across the Sandhills. Uncountable threads of milkweed silk and their attached seeds would be sailing over the prairie, seeking out the perfect place to settle and take root.

Snow Blows like Spirits in the Sun

Lakota elders have referred to the first moon of the new year as the "Hunger Moon" or "Moon of Popping Trees." The Cheyennes have called it the "Strong Cold Moon," and the Osages "Light-of-Day Returns." But the most powerful physical descriptor might be the Arapahos' "Snow Blows like Spirits in the Sun."

Winters in the Sandhills don't typically feature deep snows, but scouring winds whip across the dunes, sending snow crystals and sand swirling into the opaque sky. Stories abound of early home-steaders driven crazy by the keening winds and of range riders and schoolchildren becoming disoriented and freezing to death in blinding blizzards.

In Nebraska people still talk about the blizzard of 1949, when drifts higher than rooftops blocked rural roads for six weeks, and the "Schoolchildren's Storm" of 1888, when dozens of stranded farmers, ranchers, and elementary school children perished.

For indigenous people who subsisted on bison and other game, winters may have been less traumatic. Bison herds congregated in the Missouri River valley in late spring, when the tall grasses were just greening up. But to remain upright, tall grasses require large concentrations of silica, and they become indigestible by mid-summer. So the bison drifted west, where the short grasses, especially blue grama and buffalo grass, remain palatable year-round.

In the Sandhills, scattered bison herds probably lingered throughout the fall and into winter. In addition to freshly killed bison, Plains Indians subsisted throughout early winter on dried meat and pemmican, a highly nutritious mixture of bison meat, bison fat, and pounded chokecherries.

The Pawnee and Ponca peoples, who inhabited the Niobrara and Loup River valleys, located their villages in sheltered canyons, where concentrated game populations and year-round springs made life a little easier. And typically, they began each winter well stocked with squash, corn, and dried bison meat from fall hunts conducted in the shortgrass region west of the Sandhills.

Nevertheless, the most horrific story of winter suffering on the western plains involved a Plains Indian tribe, the Piegans of the Blackfoot confederacy. During the "Starvation Winter of the Blackfeet," in 1883–84, at least one-fourth of the 2,500 Piegan people died of starvation or disease.

Weather was certainly a factor, as the northern plains experienced a series of nights in January when temperatures dropped to minus forty degrees Fahrenheit, or lower, but observers reported that the winter was less severe than some previous winters. What was different was that there were no bison.

By 1883 virtually all the bison on the northern plains had been killed by market hunters. Plains people took to hunting other game, but soon most of the deer and rabbits were gone as well. Promised federal provisions barely trickled in or were never even shipped, despite pleas from reservation residents and the irascible but persistent reservation agent, John Young.

When suffering on the reservation finally led to Young's being replaced in late winter by the more sympathetic and popular Major John Allen, hundreds of people were already sick and starving. In *Blackfoot Lodge Tales*, published in 1892, ethnographer George Bird Grinnell described what confronted Allen when he arrived at the villages:

> In his efforts to learn exactly what was their condition, Major Allen one day went into 23 houses and lodges to see for himself what the Indians had to eat. In one house a rabbit was boiling in a pot. The man had killed it that morning, and it was being cooked for a starving child. In another lodge, the hoof of a steer was cooking— only the hoof—to make soup for the family. In the 23 lodges Major Allen visited that day the little rabbit and the steer's hoof were all the food he found.

As he left the last house, Major Allen reportedly broke down crying.

"To see so much misery, and feel myself utterly powerless to relieve it, was more than I could stand," he said.

The "Starvation Winter" was just the culmination of fifty years of suffering on the northwestern plains. Grinnell reported that smallpox and other diseases had already decimated the Blackfoot population.

In 1842–43 alone, Indians living near Fort Union "died in such numbers that the men of the fort were kept constantly at work digging trenches in which to bury them, and when winter came, and the ground froze so hard that it was no longer practicable to bury the dead, their bodies were stacked up like cordwood in great piles awaiting the coming of spring."

A renewed wave of European American settlers had arrived in 1860, bringing deadly measles and toxic whiskey with them. Blackfoot numbers had been reduced by more than half long before 1883.

So no, it wasn't really the weather that caused the "Starvation Winter." The combination of callous slaughter of the bison combined with a deliberate attempt to displace or annihilate indigenous peoples enabled this tragedy.

Prairie winters can prove challenging under any circumstances, but for people who understood the land and its gifts, winter offered the opportunity for communion and contemplation. The Lakotas, Cheyennes, Arapahos, Pawnees, and other peoples of the western plains took advantage of dark evenings around wood fires to share stories and reflect on the passing year.

During winter, tribal artists and oral historians ornamented deer or bison hides with often-colorful pictures depicting one or more significant events from the preceding year. Sometimes the pictographs were organized in horizontal rows, other times in spirals. These "winter counts" might describe unusual weather conditions, significant hunts, or years of sickness and suffering.

Individual pictographs might show an elk being surrounded by hunters, soldiers shooting their long guns, or people dancing around a sun dance pole. While subject to various interpretations, the images triggered a dynamic narrative of the history of the community.

In 1998 Dr. Thomas Red Owl Haukaas of the Sicangu Lakotas created a written description of some of his people's pictorial winter counts. It included the following events:

> 1872–73: Metal-Horse Attack Winter. Building of the railway through hunting grounds coupled with the flood of European immigrants led to Indian retaliation.

> 1875–76: Winter They Came like Grasshoppers. Gold diggers flocked to the Black Hills even though the hills belonged to the Lakota. The U.S. Army did not enforce its treaty promise to protect Lakota property rights.

> 1900–1901: Winter of Disbelief. A U.S. agent rented out tribal land to non-Indian ranchers in spite of a tribal moratorium against land rental.

To my eye, the winter-count skins are among the most compelling works of art ever created. The story they depict ranks among humankind's most disgraceful.

At dusk the frozen lakes and ponds along the road from Lakeside shimmer in indigo light. On the western horizon, a thin red glow separates the black outlines of the dunes from a frigid purple sky.

Arriving at my campsite on the west side of Pine Lake, I'm greeted by an especially rousing owl chorus: the two great horned owl pairs hooting back and forth across the water, the long-eared pair squawking softly in the pines, and a warbling screech-owl down along the shore.

Behind, or seemingly underneath, the owl calls lies something more mysterious, a deep groaning and earthquake-like cracking complemented by an occasional high-pitched whine that seems to shoot across the frozen lake. I'm spooked for a few minutes until I realize it's just the lake's winter voice, its icepack heaving and yawing in response to the evening chill.

After a peaceful night curled up in the sleeping bag, I awake to a cold white world, with snow piled a foot deep under the pines and fog enveloping the lake. But as soon as I head out into the dunes, the snow recedes to ragged patches interspersed with spongy meadows of russet and light-brown grass.

As in early spring, walking seems almost effortless on the frozen dunes—like strolling along a gently rising and falling sidewalk. I'm surprised by the signs of life.

Canada geese honk and chortle out on the ice, while crows, robins, and juncos chatter in the pines. Wild turkey tracks wind in and out of the woods, interspersing with cottontail pellets and shallow cottontail beds. It isn't long before an audacious cottontail appears right in front of me, hopping complacently over the frozen sand.

Purple berries ornament the junipers, and I can hear a juniper solitaire warbling its winter territorial song in the distance. Bronze pine cones, still bearing seeds, lie in patches of snow. Even the highest dunes show signs of life, including recently excavated pocket gopher mounds, silvery seeds still clinging to the stems of the sand bluestem, and feathery deer mouse trails decorating the snow.

Patches of grayish-green pasture sage grow beneath the velvety red seedheads of knotweed, an edible member of the buckwheat family. A leafless, waist-high plains evening-star stalk sports a cluster of barrel-shaped carpals filled with loose, rattling seeds. I put one in my mouth, and it tastes faintly nutty.

But it's plenty raw up here, with temperatures hovering in the teens and a fresh breeze blowing out of the northwest, and the cacophony of dozens of Canada and cackling geese somewhere in the fog draws me back toward the lake.

On the way down through a patch of waist-high switchgrass, I happen upon a soft deer bed and nestle down to test it out. Seems like a cozy place to spend the night. And the deer scats in the grass must provide food for all kinds of beetles and other insects. Juniper twigs in the sand suggest that the mice and squirrels have been busy here as well.

Crunching back through the pines, I'm startled by a woodland hawk zigzagging through the trees. Off to my left, a white-breasted ferruginous hawk dips and dives over the snowy dunes.

A flock of black-capped chickadees and red-breasted nuthatches twitters by, the chickadees chattering energetically as they dangle from the tips of spider-laden cones. Ornithologists now understand that their vocal repertoire, which consists of variably pitched "chick-a-dee-dee" calls, high-pitched "see-see-see" notes, warbled winter songs, and mournful territorial "fee-bees," constitutes a complex language that binds the flock together, distinguishes it from other flocks, and protects it from danger.

A particularly long and emphatic "dee-dee-dee" call may signal the proximity of a dangerous northern pygmy-owl or woodland hawk. Shorter and less strident calls might signal a great horned owl or red-tailed hawk, since these larger predators are not as agile and thus pose less of a threat.

Other inflections and intonations transmit social messages. As I sit propped against a ponderosa pine in the midst of the flock, the "dee-dee-dees" grow more subdued. "Just another human." They know I'm here, but they also understand I probably won't harm them.

Nuthatches, brown creepers, kinglets, and woodpeckers seek chickadee flocks in winter, perhaps because the chickadees are so vigilant or because they provide safety in numbers. With the chickadees keeping an eye out for predators, the woodpeckers can hammer away at conifer trunks without constantly having to look over their shoulders. The holes they drill in the bark create foraging opportunities for the smaller birds, who also pick off flying insects escaping the woodpeckers' wrath.

Watching fluffy, half-ounce chickadees flit artfully from branch to branch while chattering exuberantly, it would be easy to conclude that they are among the most confident and content of beings. Several people have made this observation, including Cherokee elders who described black-capped chickadees as bearers of truth and knowledge who could foretell the future.

Naturalist Kathryn Armstrong expounds: "The cheerful black-capped chickadee is one of America's favorite birds. The happy sound of the 'chick-a-dee-dee' call resonates throughout our woods . . . [even] in the depths of winter when the birds have the heart and energy to serenade the world."

I felt this way, until one morning when I came upon two male chickadees strafing each other in the air and pecking and clawing on the ground, apparently fighting to the death over a territorial boundary or potential mate. Then I learned that far from being idyllic, peaceful cooperatives, chickadee flocks are hierarchical associations, where the dominant birds control many of the resources, including sex. It turns out the chickadees are among the most promiscuous of songbirds, and a few dominant males in each flock get most of the action.

As for cheerfully singing their way through winter, chickadees face mortal peril during the coldest nights. Even while huddling together in tree cavities, allowing their body temperature to drop fifteen degrees or more and shivering constantly, chickadees barely make it through. If they don't find food as soon as they arouse at dawn, they can die of hypothermia within a few hours.

Chickadees dampened by drizzle prior to the arrival of an arctic cold front stand little chance. Thanks to years of bird banding by Aldo Leopold on his farm in central Wisconsin during the 1940s, we can surmise that most young chickadees in that region probably don't survive their first winter of life. More recent bird banding studies have confirmed Leopold's observations.

In short, like so many other beings, chickadees are remarkable survivors with unique communication, social, and foraging skills. And I'm sure they experience most of the same emotions that we feel, including hunger, infatuation, maternal love, anger, fear, and yes, contentment.

So when I see a handsome black-and-white chickadee dangling from pine cones and somehow extracting enough spiders and insect eggs to replace the 30 percent of its body weight lost during the night, I feel only admiration and wonder. And after the flock has moved on, the woods do seem empty and cold.

In the meadow at the north end of the lake I stumble upon a dozen male ring-necked pheasants strutting, circling, and leaping into the air, their blood-red face patches gleaming in the sunlight. This ritualistic dance seems like another example of spring energy during the heart of winter. Or maybe, a sign of global climate change. I can't remember ever seeing pheasants displaying this early in the year. The pheasants race around helter-skelter, then vanish into the grass.

Just to my right, the frozen lake surface is a frosted mosaic of pastel blue, ivory, and slate gray, with the Canada geese standing placidly out in the middle. But most of the lake's life energy isn't visible. Under the ice, bluegills hunt minnows, beavers transport succulent willow branches into the subsurface entrances of their cozy lodges, and turtles sleep peacefully.

Beginning in December, Sandhills snapping turtles dive down to the muddy bottom, enter a state of torpor, and literally stop breathing. All the oxygen they need apparently seeps through pores in their leathery skin. Their heart rate may slow to just a few beats per minute.

These snappers drift into a state resembling suspended animation as their body temperature plummets close to freezing. But as winter deepens, oxygen levels in frozen-over ponds drop to dangerously low levels, even for barely animate beings.

Snappers respond by lowering their metabolic rates even further. This in turn causes acids to build up in their tissues, cramping their muscles. Remarkably, the torpid turtles have yet another answer; they extract calcium from their shells to neutralize the acid, much as humans use antacids to relieve heartburn.

When they emerge from their underwater haunts in early spring, their leathery, wrinkled visage reminds us of ancient dinosaurs, and for good reason. Snapping turtles have been living and evolving in North America for ninety million years, long enough to learn how to survive winter without taking a single breath.

Chorus frogs hibernate in piles of leaf litter or under logs and can freeze nearly solid. Up to 65 percent of the total body water in some frozen frogs may be ice, but they avoid ice crystal formation within critical cells, since ice crystals can cut through their cell membranes and quickly kill them.

Frogs produce alcohol glycerol and glucose, which protect their membranes when freezing does occur and restrict ice formation. Like snapping turtles, frogs can breathe through their skin, so they stay put underground, dead to the world until spring.

In the woods behind me, adult mourning cloak and hoary comma butterflies hibernate in tree crevices and under piles of leaves. Viceroy caterpillars sleep in rolled up willow leaves along the shoreline, while tiger swallowtail chrysalids resembling shards of bark dangle from cottonwood twigs.

It's mind-boggling to think of all these life forms sleeping under the water, in the muck, and in the trees. I wonder what they might be thinking, if anything. Are torpor and hibernation more like napping, dying, or an extended state of meditation?

We do know that snapping turtles often sleep with their eyes open and will arouse and swim around under the ice on sunny winter days. Hoary commas and mourning cloaks sometimes emerge from hibernation and begin flying through the woods on sunny January mornings.

I return to camp a little before noon, just as a strong breeze rushes out of the south, melting away the fog and sending little wisps of snow crystals spinning skyward. For a moment the sun peeks through, transforming the swirling crystals into sparkling diamonds.

The following morning I awake a couple of hours before dawn, as alert as a cat. Way too cold to think about reading or going out walking in the dark, I bury my face in the sleeping bag and lie awake reflecting on thirty-five years of camping alone in this peaceful prairie woodland.

I remember the first year I came here, when I watched a pair of ospreys nabbing fish from the inlet at the north end of the lake; my first nose-to-nose encounter with the white-tailed doe in the clearing behind my tent; and the year when the long-eared owls welcomed me into their world.

I remember the year right after my mother died, when the pine shadows shivered in howling winds. I recall drought years when shallow ponds in the interdunal valleys dried up and you could smell the rotting algae from miles away; wet Junes when the road up from Crescent Lake was flooded over and awash with foraging shorebirds and ducks; and the year when Nebraska Game and Parks biologists, wishing to improve the fishing, dredged what my

Caddo Indian friend described as a "hole in the lake" (not to be confused with startling and illuminating holes in the sky).

I remember a gentle wild turkey who accompanied me on morning walks, the pair of pristine white swans trumpeting their way out of the cattails at the south end of the lake one spring morning, a sleek mink posing on a half-submerged log, a lightning bolt wrapped in a rainbow within a purple-black thunderstorm.

More than anything, I feel a sense of constancy and belonging. Things have shifted slightly over time, but this seminal place looks and functions much as it did thirty-five years ago. I can only hope it will remain this way.

Popping Trees

At dawn there's a distinctive feeling of danger in the air, a brittleness and crackling stillness. Almost as soon as I put my boots on, I find myself tucking my gloved hands into the armpits of my down jacket and jumping up and down to keep my feet from going numb. Just after sunrise, a frigid breeze sweeps in from the north, sending wisps of fog racing across the frozen lake surface.

It was mornings like this one, when ice-encrusted cottonwood twigs made popping sounds at sunrise, that gave this first full month of winter another one of its names. The expression "Moon of Popping Trees" summons memories not just of cold and survival but also of one of the most tragic and unforgivable events in North American history.

Some historians have characterized the Wounded Knee Massacre, which occurred just forty-five miles north of here on December 29, 1890, as a tragic mistake; others as the violent culmination of three hundred years of conquest, annihilation, and subjugation. The proximal cause was European American overreaction to a messianic movement that had spread among tribes of the western plains after years of betrayal and broken promises.

The 1868 Treaty of Fort Laramie, which ceded all of present-day North and South Dakota along with exclusive hunting rights in the grasslands of western Nebraska to the Sioux Nation (a loose confederacy of linguistically similar groups, sometimes referred to as Lakotas, Dakotas, and Nakotas), was supposed to have resolved the conflict between European American settlers and the western tribes forever. But over the ensuing years, the federal government systematically violated the treaty, eventually carving up the Sioux Nation into a dozen small reservations.

The four largest Lakota-dominated reservations are in present-day South Dakota:

Standing Rock (Hunkpapa Sioux), just west of the Missouri River and straddling the North Dakota border.

Cheyenne River (Minneconjou Sioux), along the Missouri River in central South Dakota.

Rosebud (Brulé Sioux), west of the Missouri River and extending from the White River south to the Nebraska border.

Pine Ridge (Oglala Sioux), formerly known as Red Cloud agency, south of the Black Hills and extending west one hundred miles from Rosebud.

In 1887 the federal government passed the Dawes Act, which fractured these and other smaller reservations into 160-acre family allotments. Promised annuities and rations arrived sporadically, at best, and farming the arid land proved mostly futile. Families were broken up as children were shipped off to church-dominated boarding schools. Many of the allotted lands passed into the hands of European American ranchers.

By the late 1880s, people were desperate and starving. It was under these circumstances that the Ghost Dance movement spread across the continent. The movement had been inspired by the words of a Paiute prophet who had envisioned a paradise on earth where living and departed Native Americans could mingle in peace. The self-appointed messiah, after changing his name from Jack Wilson to Wovoka, instructed people to dance solemnly for five days each month to bring about this transformation.

When federal officials heard that some ghost dancers were wearing special shirts thought to protect them from army bullets and others were neglecting their farms, they resolved to halt the dancing. They began by trying to take some of the chiefs into custody, including Sitting Bull, a Hunkpapa Lakota most famous for his role in the defeat of General George Armstrong Custer at the 1874 Battle of Little Big Horn. His bodyguards resisted, and after a flurry of gunfire, he lay dead.

Fearing further violence, more than one hundred members

of his tribe fled the Standing Rock Reservation in north-central South Dakota and eventually joined up with Chief Si Tanka ("Spotted Elk") and his Miniconjou band at the Cheyenne River Reservation, along the Missouri River. They resolved to travel westward to the Pine Ridge reservation, along the South Dakota-Nebraska border, where Chief Red Cloud had served as an intermediary between the whites and the Indians.

When they arrived at Wounded Knee Creek, ten miles east of the agency, Si Tanka's group of 350 men, women, and children were met by close to 500 federal soldiers and instructed to camp overnight before being escorted to Pine Ridge the next day. Looking up, they saw the soldiers installing Hotchkiss artillery guns on hills overlooking their camp.

When the soldiers entered the camp the next morning, they expressed peaceful intentions but then told the people to relinquish all their rifles. A few of the men and women, believing that no rifles meant starvation and possible annihilation, hesitated, and after the troops began ransacking the peoples' lodges and possessions, a small skirmish erupted.

Before long, sounds of the initial gunshots were drowned out by the roar of artillery shells raining down on the camp. Screaming women and children ran for their lives, and some were shot down as far as three miles from the campsite.

Tim Giago, an Oglala Lakota editor and publisher of *Native Sun News*, described the slaughter: "The unarmed Lakota fought back with their bare hands. . . . Elderly men and women, unable to fight back, stood defiantly and sang their death songs before falling to the hail of bullets. The number of Lakota people murdered that day is still unknown. The mass grave at Wounded Knee holds the bodies of 150 men, women, and children."

One Lakota woman told of concealing herself and two terrified girls in a clump of bushes. She put her hands over their mouths to keep them quiet, but a soldier spotted them anyway. He fired a bullet into the head of each girl, then shot her in the stomach. She related the incident to an Indian physician at a makeshift hospital in Pine Ridge before dying, herself.

Every year since 1990, Lakota leaders have organized a trail ride to the Wounded Knee site. After arriving from 150 miles or more away, they hold a ceremony called "wiping away the tears," to remember the tragic massacre and pray for peace.

Alex White Plume, former president of the Oglala Sioux tribe, helped organize the ride on the advice of his uncle, a spiritual interpreter.

"My uncle said we had to do some grieving over the historic genocide of our people. As Lakota our whole purpose is to be free from ill feelings, trauma, guilt. But the historic genocide weighed so heavily on us that we couldn't think past it."

In 1980 the U.S. Supreme Court agreed that the U.S. government had illegally appropriated the Black Hills and surrounding grasslands from the Sioux Nation and awarded $100 million in reparations. The Sioux Nation refused the money, which with inflation, now amounts to around $1.5 billion.

"We'd like to see that land back," said Chief Spotted Tail, whose great-great-grandfather was among tribal leaders who signed the treaty.

Daniel R. Wildcat, a member of the Muscogee Nation and professor at Haskell Indian Nations University, explained why, in an online response to a 2014 article in the *Atlantic*: "Reparations are ill suited to address the harm and damage experienced by people who understand themselves, in a very practical and moral sense, as members of communities that include nonhuman life. For many Native Americans, our land (including the air, water, and biological life on which we depend) is a natural relative, not a natural resource."

Tribal leaders also have asserted that since the treaty was an agreement between two sovereign nations, restoration of the treaty should be negotiated between the U.S. government and the Sioux Nation, not determined by a U.S. judicial entity.

Restoring the Black Hills and surrounding grasslands to the Sioux Nation may not be as daunting as it may first appear, since much of this land is currently under stewardship of the federal government as national parks, national forests, and national grasslands. Remaining private holdings could be purchased one by one on a willing seller basis, just as the national grasslands were pieced together during and after the Great Depression.

In other parts of North America, significant portions of tribal lands have been restored. In 2018, after decades of negotiation, Congress finally passed the Western Oregon Tribal Fairness Act, which returned thirty-two thousand acres of stolen land to the Umpqua, Coos, and Siuslaw Indians.

Those of us who benefit from this land have an obligation to stand with its lawful owners. We can start by supporting groups such as the Native American Rights Fund and Indian Land Tenure Foundation, which continue to negotiate with the U.S. government.

Meanwhile, we might pledge to learn from the people who occupied and worshiped this land, to honor their stories and their cosmology, to begin to appreciate their sacred relationships with their homelands. Eventually we might apply that understanding to everything we do, including restoring the health of all of our precious North American ecosystems.

Among the biggest victims of the various nineteenth-century treaties were the Pawnees and Poncas, who had lived prosperously in the fertile valleys within and just east of the Sandhills. The Pawnees occupied the Republican, Platte, and Loup River valleys for more than two centuries, and the Loup River was named after their Skiri (Wolf) band. They relinquished most of their lands to the white settlers through treaties signed in 1833, 1848, and 1857 in exchange for promised and ultimately elusive annuities. The federal government eventually took what remained.

The Poncas lived in a fertile paradise near the mouth of the Niobrara River valley, an area of moist woodlands, bursting springs, and abundant game. The Treaty of Fort Laramie mistakenly awarded all their lands to the Lakotas. After a decade of conflict, the tribe was removed to "Indian Territory" in Oklahoma, a place many leaders referred to as the "country of death."

After a heroic and peaceful march back to their homeland, led by legendary Chief Standing Bear, the tribe captured the hearts of Native rights activists. They eventually won a seminal lawsuit against the federal government acknowledging their right to exist as "people" and were granted a tiny reservation where the Niobrara meets the Missouri. Their annual August powwow at this site, open to everyone, celebrates their resilience.

Before the Pawnees, Poncas, and Lakotas arrived in the region from the north, Sandhills valleys were occupied by farmers and hunters of the Central Plains tradition. These people lived in permanent villages, primarily in the river valleys, and grew corn, beans, and squash. Some of the villages contained substantial earth lodges with timber frameworks.

Woodland peoples, who lived in the region one thousand to two thousand years ago, may have been the first occupants of the Central Plains to make ceramic vessels. They grew corn and squash, hunted bison and small game, and gathered wild plants. They were preceded for six thousand years by Archaic peoples, who mostly hunted and gathered while living in rock shelters such as Ash Hollow Cave, overlooking the North Platte River near Lewellen.

All of these peoples shared a couple of attributes that distinguish them from European American explorers and settlers. First, they lived in small groups and interacted with the natural world in a relatively harmonious way. Second, they viewed themselves as part of the natural world, rather than as separate from it or in control of it.

It was the idea that human ingenuity and technology could conquer nature and bend it to our needs—along with a growth-at-all-costs philosophy that eventually became our dominant religion—that eventually got us into the mess we're in now.

It's true that activities of some previous cultures depleted some resources on the western plains. Many anthropologists believe that spear-carrying Paleoindians, who occupied the western plains eight thousand to thirteen thousand years ago, contributed to the extinction of many of the large mammals that thrived toward the end of the last ice age. Introduction of the horse from Europe during the seventeenth century created a new wave of environmental stresses as highly mobile Plains Indians became capable of killing many more large game animals than they needed for food.

But what European Americans are doing now is on a scale all its own. We've wiped out most of the prairie megafauna, including grizzly bears, wolves, and 99 percent of the wild bison and elk; tilled under 97 percent of native tallgrass prairies and more than half of shortgrass and mixed-grass prairies; depleted most natural water sources; and sprayed dangerous chemicals on the land. Clearly this isn't sustainable. The question is how we change our behavior.

I feel hopeful on a couple of fronts. First, this dangerous experiment began only a couple of hundred years ago, and it's easy to understand why it became so seductive. In 150 years, we have eliminated plagues and other fatal diseases, provided food surpluses for much of the world's population, and achieved levels of personal comfort and mobility that would have been unthinkable before industrialization. Second, global climate change, along with the COVID-19 pandemic, have triggered a powerful awareness that we will have to partner with nature, stop polluting, stop depleting natural resources, and control our numbers if we're going to survive as a species.

None of this awareness is new. Lakota chief Luther Standing Bear wrote simply: "We could feel the peace and power of the Great Mystery in the soft grass under our feet and the blue sky above us. All this made deep feeling within us, and this is how we got our religion."

Kwakiutl chief Seattle was quoted as saying: "All things are connected. Whatever befalls the earth befalls the children of the earth."

Indigenous cultures carry practical knowledge from centuries of living in nature, along with an abiding understanding of our proper role as partners in nature. Native American writers and activists have helped us understand that simply saving a few species of animals or a checkerboard array of wildlife habitat will never suffice. If we want to heal nature, we also need to heal ourselves and our relationships, transcending colonialism and shortsighted exploitation of natural resources.

Can we achieve this transformation? Here in the Sandhills, generational ranchers have learned how to make a productive living while nurturing native grasses. Enforcement of the Migratory Bird Treaty and Wetlands Protection Act, along with the creation of the national wildlife refuges and state wildlife areas, has helped birds, mammals, and other wildlife to thrive.

What's been largely left out of this equation is the people living just a few miles to the north, the legal stewards of much of this land. The more that state and local governments can partner with them, the better off we'll all become.

Huddling out of the wind on this raw winter morning just a stone's throw from Wounded Knee, it's hard to process the layers of subjugation and suffering inflicted on Native peoples by my great-great grandparents' and subsequent generations. Perhaps listening attentively and striving to treat the earth and all its inhabitants with reverence and respect qualify as first steps.

But whatever we might do, I fear we'll always carry subliminal feelings of sadness and shame while walking across these wind-buffeted hills.

Turtle Tears

It may have been the silvery glint of sunlight in his ruby-red eye that got me. Or the ornate pattern of yellow stripes on his domed carapace. Or perhaps the look of patience and quiet determination as his parrot-like beak poked out of the shell and his leathery legs dangled limply.

Hunkered down in the middle of a one-lane asphalt roadway, the turtle seemed recklessly unperturbed. I parked the Subaru on the grassy shoulder, got out, and waited for a while, listening for any vehicles that might come along before the turtle made it all the way across.

After several minutes without any obvious movement, I walked over, picked him up gently, and set him down on the far side of the road. I got peed on for my efforts, but that was about it. The turtle extended his dinosaur-like head, rose up on his gnarly, clawed forelegs, and ambled into the grass.

Since then I've seen dozens of ornate box turtles parked in the middle of the Oshkosh-Lakeside road. But the protocols among those of us who treasure wild turtles haven't changed. You stop on the shoulder, get out, and direct "traffic" until the turtle moves on. If it stays put, you gently help it across.

This early summer Sandhills ritual is one of the things that endeared me to the place from the beginning. Any highway supporting more ornate box turtles than automobiles seems almost civilized. There's even a signed mud turtle crossing at Crescent Lake National Wildlife Refuge.

But the whole routine begs a question. Why on earth—or asphalt—do these turtles feel compelled to cross the roads? Scientific observations tell us that when box turtles are breeding way up in the dunes in late spring and early summer, pairs keep pretty much to their overlapping home ranges, where the female eventually digs a hole in the sand and lays her eggs.

In drier regions of the Great Plains, ornate box turtles have been shown capable of going weeks without drinking, supplementing their mostly insect diet with juicy berries, grasses, and wildflowers. But where water is available, the turtles will make treks of up to two-thirds of a mile down to the nearest lake or pond. On especially hot days later in the summer, adults sometimes visit the same ponds to find shade or cooling mud.

I accepted this analysis without much reflection or any investigation. But after more than thirty-five years of shepherding these ancient beings across the roadway, it seemed about time to find out more first hand.

After spending a peaceful early June night sleeping out near Crescent Lake, I headed north up the one-lane strip of asphalt, bumping along at a comfortable twenty-five miles per hour. It had been the third consecutive wet year in western Nebraska, and the High Plains aquifer had risen by several feet, sufficient to inundate portions of the north-south arterials.

Less than a mile north of the refuge, I encountered a 150-yard stretch where a quarter-mile wide lake completely obscured the road. A yellow sign said simply, "Water on Roadway, 10 MPH." It could just as well have said, "Nearly Every North American Waterbird Foraging in Former Roadway."

White-faced ibis waded casually in the clear water, accompanied by American avocets, northern shovelers, willets, black-necked stilts, northern phalaropes, and great blue herons. I eased through the foot-deep water at one or two miles per hour, gently nudging the foraging birds out of the way with my wake.

They didn't seem to mind, filling back in as soon as I moved on. At one point I came upon a black-crowned night heron performing a high-wire act on the top rung of the roadside barbed-wire fence. He seemed to be searching for frogs or other prey in the clear water along the shoulder. And after a couple of minutes of teetering from foot to foot and balancing by stretching out his wings, he plunged headfirst into the water.

Scenes like this are among the deterrents to covering any distance on Sandhills roads. There's so much wildlife. A few years ago, the chair of the ecology department at the University of Colorado said he'd like to join me for a night at Pine Lake. It was his first foray into the region, and he asked me how much time he should allow to get from Oshkosh to the lake, a distance of about eighty miles.

"At least five hours," I said.

"Five hours, really?" he replied.

"Unless you see something very special," I equivocated.

"Then I might not make it up there until almost dinnertime."

I never saw him. Later he related that he had spent eight hours driving the thirty-mile stretch from Oshkosh to north of Crescent Lake, then ended up sleeping in his car. I'm guessing he encountered a good number of box turtles, as well as pronghorns, white-tailed deer, tiger beetles, scurrying kangaroo mice, green racers, avocets, and burrowing owls along the way.

With all the water flooding the interdunal meadows on this early summer morning, I didn't expect to encounter any box turtles until the road wended its way into the drier dunes a few miles north of the wildlife refuge. And sure enough, as soon as I crested the first rise, there was a big one plunked down on the asphalt.

I parked thirty yards up the road, sat on the back bumper, and watched through my binoculars. The turtle's yellow-brown eyes indicated it was a female, and the four-inch length of her carapace suggested she might be several decades old.

During the eighteenth and nineteenth centuries, people occasionally carved their initials or the date into the shells of box turtles. Some eastern box turtles captured later showed dates indicating they were more than one hundred years old. Unfortunately, there's no way of authenticating this cruel manner of aging box turtles, but individuals in captivity routinely live more than forty years.

No one seems to know why turtles and tortoises live so long, but slow growth, slow metabolisms, and relatively stress-free lives may contribute to their longevity. Their slower metabolisms enable them to survive weeks without water, and their natural protection from predators and penchant for hibernating several months of the year allow them to take their time reproducing. Most ornate box turtles don't reach sexual maturity until they're about ten years old.

The box turtles' hinged plastron (the lower portion of the shell) enables them to completely retreat inside when danger approaches, so they have little to fear from most predators. Collisions with automobiles may cause more deaths than all the predators combined.

The wild pet trade also has taken a toll on ornate box turtle populations. Hundreds of thousands of box turtles are sold each year, and ornate box turtles do poorly in captivity, often dying within a few months after adoption. Exotic diseases brought in by imported Asian box turtles threaten wild populations.

A related turtle species found in the central and eastern Sandhills, Blanding's turtle, has become threatened by both the wild pet trade and automobile traffic. While its North American range centers in the Great Lakes region and extends into Ontario and New England, this shy, semiaquatic turtle appears to be making its last stand in the Sandhills, where roads are far enough apart to give it a chance. The one hundred thousand or so Blanding's turtles remaining in the Sandhills may exceed the number found throughout the rest of their North American range.

Volunteers working to construct wildlife culverts under Sandhills roadways quickly fall in love with these mostly gray, ten-inch-long turtles due in part to the way their bright yellow throats and long, curving beaks create the impression they are perpetually smiling. Construction of culverts and impermeable roadside fences along U.S. 83 south of Valentine has paid off, with "only" one-fourth of observed turtles being crushed by vehicles, as opposed to nearly two-thirds previously.

Like ornate box turtles, Blanding's turtles can live up to fifty years or more. But they didn't evolve to deal with trucks and cars racing along highways at seventy-five miles per hour. Outside the Nebraska Sandhills, habitat fragmentation has become too great and roads too numerous to give them much of a chance.

People sometimes equate long life with great wisdom, and cultures around the world have celebrated the wisdom of turtles. The name Turtle Island, used by many Native American peoples to describe what Europeans later referred to as North America, evolved from origin stories common to Algonquin- and Iroquoian-speaking peoples.

Some of these stories begin with the image of a flooded earth occupied by a few aquatic animals and a supernatural being, *Nanabush*, capable of creating life. He asks the animals to swim down deep and gather soil that can be used to create the new world. After several animals try and fail, a muskrat finally emerges on the surface with some wet soil in its paws.

Nanabush takes the soil and puts it on the back of a floating turtle. This island of life grows and grows, until it becomes the center of all creation.

Other versions, related by Anishinaabe peoples of the Northeast and Upper Midwest, begin in the Sky World and describe the terrifying fall of pregnant Sky Woman through a hole under the roots of a tree. As she plummets down, birds guide her onto a turtle's back. A muskrat brings up mud from the depths of a vast ocean, the earth and a garden of plants grow around her, and Turtle Island comes to life.

Turtles date back more than two hundred million years, when ocean-dwelling individuals with hard shells and giant flippers measured ten feet long and weighed up to two tons. Fifteen-million-year-old fossils of box turtles similar in appearance to modern species have been uncovered in western Nebraska. Ornate box turtles (*Terrapene ornata*) have been around for least five million years.

There's something else about turtles that makes them appear wise. As they move slowly across the landscape, apparently secure inside their snuggly engineered shells, they seem almost serene and unafraid of people.

Their moist, unblinking eyes convey patience and mystery. Peering closely at the eye of a female, you can see a black pupil with yellow lines radiating out like sunlight through a liquid brown iris. In snapping turtles, the yellow markings flare out like the fiery corona of a dark star.

While land turtles don't shed tears as prolific as those of sea turtles, they still excrete liquid from their eyes. These "turtle tears" play on our emotions, while also attracting butterflies and other insects who sip up the salty nectar. From an early age, we're programmed to respond to tearful eyes with nurturing feelings. Though we may not be able to speak directly to turtles, they speak to us.

After a few minutes, my turtle stuck out her head and began to wobble toward the edge of the road. I strolled in that direction, carrying my binoculars, and arrived just as she shot through the roadside grass and scurried down an embankment. I was shocked by her sudden speed.

She created a little tunnel in the grass as she proceeded down the hill and across a wet meadow speckled with lavender penstemons and pinkish-white spearmint. I lost sight of her for several minutes as she plodded through a stand of eight-foot-high cattails, but I saw the cattails quivering and heard soft crunching sounds.

She emerged onto a gentle rise on the far edge of the cattails and descended to the edge of a shallow lake. She settled down in the muck and lowered her head into the water.

After twenty minutes or so without further signs of movement, I grew weary of standing in the sun watching and strolled up and down the roadway, admiring the yellow-headed blackbirds singing hoarsely from swaying cattail stalks. When I returned to my observation point, the turtle had vanished.

I waited a while longer but saw no more sign of her. I could only imagine her thrashing back through the cattails, plodding up through the concealing tall grasses, crossing the treacherous roadway, and then inching her way back up to her nesting territory in the dunes. After eventually finding the perfect spot to scrape out a hole with her hind legs, she'd lay a half dozen white eggs with brittle shells.

If the nest were just a few inches deep and nevertheless escaped predation, inch-long hatchlings would dig their way out in late summer or early fall, scurry a short distance across the dunes, and find a safe place in the sand to hole up until spring. If the nest were deeper, the hatchlings might simply burrow down farther into the sand to hibernate below the nest, waiting until May for their first glimpse of sunlight.

Either way, they'd emerge into a near-perfect turtle world—with soft sand for hiding and sleeping; grassy hollows full of caterpillars, crickets, and succulent wildflowers; and spring-fed ponds just a short trek away.

Circles of Life

I was sitting at my lakeside picnic table one May morning twenty-five years ago when I looked up and saw a small wild turkey trotting out of the pines. I froze in place, thinking she probably hadn't seen me yet. But she kept on coming, and before I knew it she was standing a few feet away, casually pecking at food scraps scattered in the grass.

This was my first encounter with a wild turkey at the lake, and I ran into the woods, where my friend Roger was still asleep in his tent, imploring him to come down to the picnic area to see the turkey. He stuck his head out of the tent flap and muttered, "I don't need to, Steve. Look behind you." She was standing just a few feet away.

I named her Roxanne, after the heroine in *Cyrano de Bergerac*, and over the next two years we became a tight couple. Every time I arrived at the lake, I'd look for Roxanne. Sometimes she wouldn't appear for a day or two; other times she would trot right down to my car and greet me with purring clucks.

We'd take long walks together through the woods and around the lake, with Roxanne often wandering off or lagging behind but typically scurrying up to me whenever I stopped. One morning, as I was packing to head home, I caught her poking around in the back compartment of the Subaru. During our first morning together, I photographed her hunkered down in Roger's lap while he stroked her neck feathers.

Having a semi-feral wild turkey as a frequent companion added spice to my visits. But I knew there was something not right with this situation, and I wasn't too surprised when she disappeared after a couple of years, a likely victim of a hunter or coyotes.

I later found out that Roxanne, along with another female I discovered incubating a large clutch of brown-speckled eggs in a patch of switchgrass near the southern lakeshore, had most likely been released by an area rancher. The rancher had raised a clutch of wild turkeys in her barn and then let them go. Obviously, at least one of the turkeys had imprinted on her surrogate mother.

At the beginning of the twentieth century, the remaining North American wild turkey population stood at only a few tens of thousands. These wily and beautiful birds, once described by Benjamin Franklin as a better national symbol than the bald eagle (which he referred to as "a bird of bad moral character") had nearly been extirpated by overhunting and loss of woodland habitat.

Early efforts at reintroduction failed because the turkeys imprinted on their human caretakers, losing their fear of people and other potential predators. During the late twentieth century, wildlife conservationists developed new protocols for rearing and reintroduction that required stewards to feed the turkeys without having personal contact with them.

North American populations took off, and now close to ten million wild turkeys roam the woodlands and farmlands of the United States and Canada. Throughout the Midwest and Great Plains, it's not unusual to see them strolling down main streets of rural communities.

After my last encounter with Roxanne at Pine Lake, I didn't see another wild turkey there for close to ten years. But now I see or hear them virtually every time I visit. The difference is that these are warier birds, and they usually scurry off into the woods when I walk by.

While more and more wild vertebrates find their way onto endangered species lists, several are making impressive recoveries in the Sandhills. Elk, which were wiped out from western Nebraska and all of the plains by market hunters during the late nineteenth century, now bugle each fall in the North Platte River valley downstream from Oshkosh and along the Niobrara River as far east as Ainsworth.

River otters, mostly descendants of a few dozen released into Sandhills streams by Nebraska Game and Parks biologists during the 1980s, now thrive in the Niobrara, Loup, and North Platte Rivers. When I sleep out along the North Platte, I hear the otters splashing in the water and conversing in clicking, mechanical tones throughout the night.

Bald eagles nest at Crescent Lake and Valentine national wildlife refuges, and six hundred thousand migrating Sandhill cranes gather each March along the Platte River in central Nebraska. Trumpeter swans have recovered from near oblivion, with more than a thousand inhabiting Sandhills lakes and wetlands. White-faced ibis and black-crowned night herons have become common throughout the region.

Semi-wild bison herds graze at Fort Niobrara National Wildlife Refuge and the Nature Conservancy's Niobrara Valley Preserve. A few mountain lions and black bears prowl the forested ridges of Oglala National Grassland, in northwestern Nebraska, and one or two have even wandered into Ash Hollow State Historical Park, along the North Platte River.

So which species are we losing? For starters, invasion of lakes and ponds by Asian carp, deliberately introduced tiger muskies, and exotic species of algae and pondweed threaten native fish populations, nesting trumpeter swans (the tiger muskies pick off the cygnets, one by one), and native leopard frogs. Warming of pond waters as global climate change progresses could exacerbate these trends.

Loss of naturally occurring areas of bare sand—a result of fire suppression, elimination of bison, and modern grazing practices—threatens several species that are endemic to sand dune environments, including piping plover and Hayden's blowout penstemon.

Ranchers and managers of wildlife refuges have done a commendable job preserving the Sandhills prairie and its associated rivers and lakes. However, suppression of fire and elimination of free-roaming bison herds throughout the area has led to a disturbing trend. Throughout the Sandhills, exotic trees—especially red cedar, green ash, Russian olive, and crack willow—dot the landscape. Like an invading army, they march steadily westward, creeping over ridgetops and encircling lakes and ponds.

Most people see this as a good thing. As a species, humans

evolved in the savannas of Africa, and trees helped nourish us, providing shade, fruit and acorns, wood for fires, and homes for prey species. So we have a natural affinity for trees.

I have an affinity for grasslands, partially, I believe, because it was only when we moved out of the forest and into the grasslands that my species really thrived. More tangibly, I love the glowing light, boundless vistas, and feelings of freedom that come with prairie landscapes. And I also understand that many of the other species that inhabit grasslands are seriously threatened by the tree invasion.

In addition to providing homes for nest predators such as starlings, blue jays, and fox squirrels, the trees support a suite of human commensal species, such as great horned owls, red-tailed hawks, and raccoons, who prey on grassland specialists. The trees also carve up the prairie into ever smaller fragments that provide insufficient space for native mammals and birds.

White-tailed jackrabbits have vanished throughout areas of the western plains that have been invaded by deciduous trees. Greater prairie-chickens and burrowing owls simply won't nest if they see trees or telephone poles nearby. During my first few years camping at Pine Lake, I occasionally saw both species in the grassy dunes west of the pines. Not anymore, or at least very rarely.

The prairie-chickens do seem to be holding their own in areas of the Sandhills that have remained nearly treeless, including Valentine National Wildlife Refuge. During April and May, you can reserve a photographic blind beside one of several dozen refuge leks, areas of relatively short or trampled-down grass where greater prairie-chickens perform their ritualistic courtship dances.

The experience is transcendent. You wake up in the dark and walk toward the blind in the moonlight, accompanied by the chirruping of chorus frogs, the "oonk-a-lunks" of courting American bitterns, and an eerie winnowing sound produced overhead as the air rushes through the tail feathers of diving Wilson's snipes.

Remembering that the snipes' winnowing stimulated the Plains Indians' celebratory ululations, it's impossible not to think, "This is the way it used to be, and the way it should remain."

As first light touches the lek, males plop down, crouch, extend their wings, inflate bright-yellow air sacs on their throats, and cackle while stomping, strutting, and careening over the grass, performing a dance that Plains Indians copied and still dance today. Every once in a while, a watching female will pick out a male and they'll wander off into the grass to mate.

A half hour or so after the sun clears the eastern horizon, all the birds rise up and disperse in a whirlwind of cackling voices and fluttering wings. The prairie grasses bask in glowing light as the still air hums with the sounds of insects waking up to the new day.

It's hard to experience this spectacle without feeling a tingle in the spine, realizing you're witnessing something one hundred times older than the Sandhills themselves, and understanding that sacred rituals like this one are becoming ever harder to find.

And we need them desperately. They provide us not only with joy and beauty but also with feelings of reassurance. We belong out here, among the prairie-chickens, bitterns, and winnowing snipes.

Many of us also long for a more gentle and holistic relationship with the natural world. We're beginning to understand that we need to start out by discarding the long-held belief that we are separate from nature and from other beings.

We're all constructed from similar DNA, and we all descended from the first one-celled creatures to inhabit the earth three billion years ago. We breathe the same air, drink the same water, and experience similar emotions of love, fear, tenderness, and wonder.

When I hear the Pine Lake coyotes howling at dawn, I recognize the voices of my ancestors. When I see a female long-eared owl peering down from her nest, I feel my mother's loving gaze. And when I see a wood duck cruising across a glassy inlet with a dozen fluffy young trailing behind her, I understand that the world is a sacred and nurturing place.

Throughout the world, indigenous peoples are spreading awareness that all of nature has rights. After Ecuador passed its law acknowledging the rights of natural beings to exist and flourish, Bolivia passed a similar constitutional amendment. Here in the United States, dozens of communities, including Santa Monica, Pittsburgh, and Crestone, Colorado, have passed rights of nature resolutions and ordinances.

In Oklahoma, the Ponca tribe passed a rights of nature resolution, then joined other Oklahoma tribes in petitioning the state government to restore their treaty-given sovereignty over the eastern half of the state. The Supreme Court reviewed the case and concluded that the tribes were entitled to environmental stewardship of much of this region, including regulation of hydraulic fracturing operations.

For thousands of years, indigenous peoples have integrated their respect for other beings into cosmologies that use circles, or hoops, to portray our relationship with sacred Earth. Native Americans use hoop inscriptions and designs to depict circles of life and the Four Directions, the Four Stages of Life, the Four Sacred Elements, and the Four Seasons. The hoops are said to have no beginning or ending and can encompass the Sun, Moon, Earth, and Stars; family and friends; all beings; or paths of energy flow.

Among European cultures, hoop imagery appears in Maypole dances, prayer circles, and rings, though we tend to forget its cultural significance. I think of my mother's wedding band, which I treasured for a decade before passing it along to a nephew so he could place it on the finger of his bride.

In *The Hoop and the Tree*, Chris Hoffman explains how these visions of Earth relationships can restore and heal: "To be fully developed, we must become ecological beings. True psychological and spiritual healing involves establishing not only right relationships with other people but also right relationships with all of the ecosystem, and, ultimately, with all of existence."

Sandhills ranchers and other residents already incorporate many of these feelings into their daily lives. That's largely because this is one of the last intact landscapes in North America, a place where human activities haven't completely transformed the natural world. Throughout the Sandhills you can still feel the flow of wildness and experience intimate natural relationships on a daily basis.

At Pine Lake, I feel hoop energy in the fresh water trickling and bubbling up from the dark aquifer, creating this cool oasis of thriving life. At night the lake surface reflects the swirling stars, whose rotation mirrors the turning of the earth and reminds me that we are one tiny speck in a boundless universe. The pines encircling the lake provide shelter and nourishment for my extended family of beings, including the owls, white-tailed deer, and wild turkeys who visit my campsite. The grassy hills rolling and tumbling toward the circular horizon bring feelings of freedom and endless possibility.

Being here feels like going back in time. For nearly two million years, humans interacted quietly with the natural world—hunting, fishing, farming, and worshiping—without dominating or destroying it. Modern agriculture and the Industrial Revolution changed all this, and somewhere along the way, we forgot how to live.

It seems a cataclysmic jump from African aborigines stalking silently through the grass or Arapaho women singing reverently to prairie turnips, to wildlife safaris and factory farms. We've all but lost the sense of peace and belonging that comes from interacting quietly with nature.

Getting it back will require some changes in our daily lives, but we will reap huge benefits, including making the world a more peaceful and healthy place. In time we may begin to appreciate wild turkeys, prairie-chickens, and prairie winds as sacred partners— rather than as two-dimensional and barely animate curiosities.

By way of preparation, we might listen again to the advice of the prescient tribal leader who lived just a few dozen miles from the place I call Pine Lake, 150 years ago. His words, as reported by nineteenth-century ethnographer John Neihardt in *Black Elk Speaks*, seem particularly relevant now: "Peace comes within the souls of men when they realize their oneness with the Universe, when they realize it is really everywhere, it is within each one of us."

After watching the sunset from high atop the Black Hills, Black Elk exulted:

> Then I was standing on the highest mountain of them all, and round about beneath me was the whole hoop of the world. And while I stood there I saw more than I can tell and I understood more than I saw; for I was seeing in a sacred manner the shapes

of all things in the spirit, and the shape of all shapes as they must live together like one being.

And I saw that the sacred hoop of my people was one of many hoops that made one circle, wide as daylight and as starlight, and in the center grew one mighty flowering tree to shelter all the children of one mother and one father. And I saw that it was holy.

Path of Souls

After camping out for more than three hundred nights at the lake, I sometimes wake up in the morning with the nagging feeling that something is eluding me. I've seen families of wood ducks cruising and flying by my campsite every summer but never found one of their cavity nests. After I surprised the mink fishing off a crooked log in the north inlet one spring morning, I never saw her again or deduced where her family might be denning. I've heard barn owls hissing and screaming at night but discovered no nest burrows in the embankments along the road east of the lake.

The expansive and mostly inaccessible wetland at the south end of the lake pulls me like a magnet. Here I've stumbled upon a wild turkey nest with eggs and documented the first nesting swamp sparrows reported in this part of western Nebraska. I encountered a pair of trumpeter swans that one March morning but never saw them again. And despite watching regionally threatened short-eared owls course over the cattails on a couple of spring mornings, I've never located one of their ground nests or their young.

This cattail marsh is among the largest I've encountered in the Sandhills, stretching for more than a mile along Pine Creek and dotted with little ponds, sloughs, and sedge-rush meadows. It must hold wonders I haven't even conceived of.

But most of the marsh lies on a private ranch, and I'm shy about imposing myself on hard-working ranchers. And even then, it's doubtful that camping within the marsh would be feasible or enjoyable, what with the boggy conditions and mosquitoes.

So, on the cusp of autumn, I'm headed toward a stately ponderosa pine on a dune overlooking the marsh to do what birdwatchers refer to as a "big sit." The term evolved out of the practice, known as a "big day," of racing all over the country searching for rare species. Some of us would rather sit and sleep out than chase.

As I walk toward the dune top a few hours before sunset, a great horned owl flies out of one of the pines and glides to shore, where a kingfisher rattles its way from one box elder limb to another. Farther out, a family of wood ducks cruises across the surface. A western grebe extends its long white neck, cocks its black-crowned head, and plunges into the depths.

Just north of where I intend to camp, a small grove of fifty-foot-tall ponderosa pines has been uprooted and toppled recently, most likely by a tornado or microburst during an August thunderstorm. Fair warning for solo campers. Otherwise, the lake appears as always, with gentle waves lapping the near shore, a dozen American white pelicans swooping and soaring over the blue water, and a lone fishing skiff cruising toward the north inlet.

I lay a beach towel, some pillows, my binoculars, various provisions, and several field guides out on a bed of soft green grass and settle in. Silvery seedheads of sand bluestem toss and sway in the breeze, while patches of curing switchgrass glow crimson in the late afternoon light. Overhead, two common nighthawks dip and dive as opaque clouds of mosquitoes swirl up from the marsh. A couple of large monarch butterflies flit by, heading in the general direction of Michoacán.

I hear several grass crickets trilling away to the right and a tree cricket chirping in the ponderosa branches overhead. Assuming it's a snowy tree cricket, the most abundant chirper in this habitat, I count twenty-eight chirps in thirteen seconds and add forty, getting a total of sixty-eight. The thermometer on my waist pack reads seventy degrees Fahrenheit.

That's quite a feat of temperature reporting for a lust-crazed creature weighing less than a gram. So how do they pull it off? They make the chirps by rubbing a file-like membrane on one wing against a "scraper" on the other wing, much as a cellist rubs a bow against pliant strings. Being cold-blooded, they can't maintain a steady body temperature. As the outside temperature warms, so do their muscles, enabling them to move their wings more rapidly. Scientific studies have determined that females are most attracted to the fastest chirping males.

These crickets are called "snowy" because of their nearly white appearance, and they are among about twenty tree cricket species (members of the genus *Oencanthus*) in North America. Different species have slightly different cadences that vary with temperature, so we can't rely exclusively on the formula in the *Farmer's Almanac*, which tends not to differentiate one tree cricket species from another.

But however the crickets do it, their rhythmic chirping engenders feelings of peace and well-being. Nathaniel Hawthorne characterized the sound as "audible stillness." When I close my eyes, I sense the pulsing heartbeats of a patient universe.

The first large visitor of interest is a striking black-and-white osprey, who flies in from the south and circles over the lake searching for fish. Every few seconds he hovers, flapping his wings rapidly, but I never see him actually dive.

He's joined in the air a few minutes later by an adult female and a rusty-tailed juvenile, suggesting that the family may have nested somewhere nearby. On the western plains, ospreys often place their nests on rural telephone poles near water, so there are certainly nesting opportunities up and down the lake-filled Pine Creek valley.

From far across the marsh, a northern harrier comes cruising low over the cattails, tilting its wings from side to side while listening for rustling meadow voles. As it sails closer, I notice its reddish-brown breast feathers, a characteristic of recently fledged youngsters.

Northern harriers build their platform nests on the ground, and the nests are almost impossible to see among surrounding waist-high grasses or head-high cattails. The one time I stumbled upon a nest while tromping through a marsh, I was mortified at the sight of two scrawny, half-grown young glaring up at me with rasping, gaping beaks. I wasn't sure whether they thought I was about to feed them or eat them, but I got out of there as fast as I could and felt a sinking feeling in my stomach for much of the morning.

Now when we train volunteers to monitor nesting harriers, we ask them to do so from several hundred yards away from the suspected nest site. We've found that we can use behavioral cues to confirm nest locations.

Harriers are polygynous, and males keep busy bringing in food to two or more incubating females, and later, a half dozen, or more, recently fledged young. The males usually drop their prey items right above each nest, with the female flying up to snatch the mouse or vole from midair. We can guess when the recently hatched young have moved off the nest by the way both adults begin carrying food to different locations within the marsh.

Numbers of nesting harriers have diminished on the western plains, where human-adapted predators, especially coyotes and red-tailed hawks, have learned to find their nests in ever more fragmented patches of marsh. So it's always exhilarating to see a juvenile harrier flying over a protected and thriving wetland.

No short-eared owls, though, at least this evening. But since they nest in the same kinds of marshes and grasslands as the harriers, they may breed here from time to time. While they have become rare throughout the western plains, scattered pairs do continue to nest in wet meadows and marshes from the central United States clear to northern Canada and Alaska.

Global warming seems to be shifting their breeding range northward. Throughout Nebraska researchers have reported only eight nesting confirmations (occupied nests or recently fledged young) since the early 1960s. In neighboring Colorado, numbers of observed nests declined by more than 50 percent over twenty years. I'll keep looking, waiting, and hoping.

As the sun eases its way down through the orange cumulus clouds to the west and the cool night air settles over the lake, the tree cricket stops chirping and the great horned owls in the nearby pines begin hooting back and forth. An intermittent shrieking in the ponderosa directly overhead indicates they still have a dependent youngster, desperate to be fed.

Off in the meadow to the right, the local coyote clan greets the sunset with a rousing chorus of yips and squeals, and as dusk settles in, there's a single hoot from a long-eared owl way off in the woods. Bats swoop over the still, gray water just out from shore, and tiny, slow-flying mosquitoes begin to home in on my exposed ears.

Then here come the stars, first brilliant Saturn high in the west, then chair-like Cassiopeia in the east, dazzling red Arcturus low in the south, and the Big Dipper draped over the northern horizon.

A half hour later, the Path of Souls, a breathtaking braided river of stars, arches across the sky. Looking up through the binoculars, I can see layer upon layer of twinkling lights, from the brightest constellations to clusters consisting of thousands of distant stars discernible only as milky white wisps.

Astronomers tell us that when we look at the Milky Way, what we're seeing is an edge-on view of our galaxy, and the brightest clouds of stars appear when we gaze toward the center. They also tell us that our galaxy is one of at least three hundred billion in our universe, an unfathomable expanse of energy and light. Even knowing all this, it's hard to imagine how anyone could experience the spectacle of the Milky Way without concluding that it is something very sacred, maybe even a pathway toward heaven.

So it was that the Inca people described the Milky Way as a river flowing through the sky that the souls of the dead follow on their way to the upper world. Similarly, Aztec creation stories portray it as a path through the wilderness of stars.

The Pawnees, who lived in the Loup River valleys of the eastern Sandhills during the eighteenth and nineteenth centuries, have referred to the Milky Way as both "buffalo dust" and the pathway of departed spirits. In *Oglala Religion*, published in 1975, anthropologist William K. Powers reported that residents of the Pine Ridge Reservation in southwestern South Dakota attributed the points of light in the Milky Way to the campfires of ghosts traveling the road to the afterlife.

Many other North American peoples, from the Senecas of the northeastern United States to the Kwakiutl of the Pacific Northwest, have expressed similar beliefs. Could it be that these beliefs developed in Asia or Beringia (in present-day western Alaska), before Asian American peoples found a navigable route through ice-age glaciers and dispersed southward throughout North and South America fifteen thousand years ago? Or do these parallel beliefs simply represent the conclusion that almost anyone might come to after gazing in awe at the river of milky white lights arching across the heavens?

I'm content imagining that these stars do, indeed, represent the campfires of our departed loved ones. They bring such glowing tranquility on these calm prairie nights, reminding me that we live in a universe that is boundless, mysterious, and full of magic. This seems a time in our human history when, more than ever, we could use some magic.

Now ensconced in my sleeping bag, I watch brilliant Deneb drift in and out of a gossamer cloud straight overhead and listen to the murmurs of ducks and geese down in the inlet. I recall my mother's stories about stargazing in San Francisco, where she worked as a commercial artist during the Second World War.

From time to time, the air raid sirens would go off, and all the city lights would flicker out. She and her roommate would climb up to the rooftop of their Marina District apartment building and sit admiring the darkened city, the foaming waves crashing against a blackened shoreline, and the searchlights scanning back and forth.

After the searchlights dimmed and before the city lights came back on, they would sit in silence, dazzled by stars. My mother described the experience—their rare glimpse of a nightly occurrence that our ancestors considered sacred beyond description—as peaceful and exhilarating. In the midst of an air raid, the stars helped her and her roommate feel safe.

My parents shared their love of the night sky with me and my two brothers during camping trips to the Oregon Cascades, pointing out the prominent constellations and describing the origins of their names. My father even ordered a primitive telescope kit from a mail order catalog and assembled it for us.

Within a generation, this basic star knowledge seems to have faded away. Now, deprived of the nightly spectacle, we tend to turn our backs on the cosmos that spawned us and nurtures us. The world can become a lonely and frightening place when we lose touch with our origins.

After an hour or so, the stars over Pine Lake begin to melt away as a silvery radiance brightens the eastern sky. The four-day-old harvest moon comes up orange and slightly lumpy, gradually illuminating the somber pines, flowing grasses, and still water. I drift off to sleep swaddled in moonlight.

I awake at dawn to a faint, tinny "ko-honking" far in the distance. This is the call I've been subconsciously yearning to hear, and I cup my ears, listening intently. But that's it, nothing more.

After I crawl out of the tent, I spend a couple of hours propped up against the ponderosa pine, scanning the vast wetland intermittently with my binoculars, but don't detect even a flash of white among the cattails. Are the swans in there somewhere, or did I imagine the sound?

By now the autumn sunlight has begun to warm the still air, and the thought of a hot cup of chai has strong appeal. As I shoulder my pack and swish back through the knee-high grasses, the white-tailed doe who confronted me during my breeding bird survey poses on the nearest dune, snorting disdainfully. I guess some relationships take time and studied patience to fully mature.

Grace

While Sandhills Decembers can trend toward cold and windy, there's often a stretch between Thanksgiving and Winter Solstice when daytime highs remain well above freezing and nighttime lows hover in the teens and low twenties. With the hunting season waning and ice fishing just beginning, there's rarely anyone camping at Pine Lake.

On the evening of the full moon, the one-lane road from Crescent Lake to Lakeside appears as deserted as I've ever seen it, without a single vehicle the whole way. North of Lakeside, where the primitive road morphs into an equally empty two-lane highway, the dunes begin to glisten with snow. All the lakes and ponds along the roadside lie under a blanket of wind-sculpted drifts and opalescent, blue ice.

At the long-abandoned one-room schoolhouse twenty miles north of Lakeside, the snow lies nearly a foot deep. Stopping to photograph the golden reflection of the setting sun in the stucco building's rectangular, wood-framed windows, I wonder what it must have been like to trudge through snow drifts and howling winds to attend this little school, miles from the nearest town.

A couple of miles farther up the road, a flock of wild turkeys scratches and gobbles in the snow-covered yard of the historic Orr family ranch house, a cozy, one-story stucco building encircled by arching cottonwoods.

At Pine Lake the frosted, marine-blue surface ice glows in lustrous evening light. Jagged cracks wending through scattered patches of half-melted snow suggest that the ice is still in the process of firming up. Here and there along shore, clumps of bronze cattails poke up through the drifts.

After plowing through a barely navigable stretch of untracked entrance road, I bounce into a lakeside clearing and step into the reassuring sounds of great horned and long-eared owls hooting up the moon. Down toward the south end of the lake, flocks of geese honk and cackle.

It's one of those big bold moons that "you can read the newspaper by" (though I can't imagine who would want to during these disturbing times), and there's no need for a headlamp while setting up the tent on an area of crusty snow under the pines. However, some melatonin might have come in handy, what with more than fourteen hours to go before sunrise.

Snuggled in my winter sleeping bag in the dark quiet of the tent, I think about the year past and what might lie ahead. The crisp night air hums with soothing energy. I imagine the last withered chokecherries dropping to the ground, winter herds of white-tailed deer circling in the moonlight, and pocket gophers retreating deep into their burrows to nibble quietly on grass roots while awaiting the first stirrings of spring. This seems like a good time to huddle up and embrace the cold and darkness, letting go of lingering agendas or regrets.

At dawn, the pines and leafless cottonwoods pose in soft blue light, creating a mood of watchful stillness. As I crunch through the cottonwood grove south of my campsite, nothing much seems to stir, save for a pair of crows flapping by. But the southeastern sky blushes rose-pink, and off in that direction the voices of the geese begin to amplify with restless energy.

Just beyond the last picnic table and the forlorn wooden outhouse, I trudge up a low ridge of connected dunes overlooking the frozen lake surface, catch my breath, and stand in awe. At least a thousand Canada and cackling geese paddle around in a circular opening in the ice and gather in groups on the edge of the water, periodically taking off in V-shaped flocks and spiraling toward the crimson clouds above the rising sun.

Looking at the geese crowded together in the water, it appears that two are snow white, not surprising given the recent resurgence in snow goose populations throughout North America. I lift my binoculars anyway, focus, lower them as the lenses fog over, then slowly raise them and focus again. They're trumpeter swans—a pair of magnificent white adults with their two full-grown, silvery-gray cygnets.

For the next two hours the trumpeter family paddles lazily across the open water, intermingling but not interacting with the geese. Occasionally one lowers its head to drink, but they never seem to feed on anything. Maybe they're content simply luxuriating in this improbable waterfowl spa.

As for nesting, they must have accomplished that the previous spring and summer in the marsh at the south end of the lake and then ventured out here to enjoy the open water without human distraction. But it's still astonishing to find them here now. I've seen swans visiting Sandhills lakes in late February as the ice begins to thaw, but never in December.

The vast majority of the several thousand lakes and ponds in the Sandhills lie in closed basins, separate from flowing rivers and creeks, and most freeze over entirely by early December. Pine Lake, with its constant influx of fifty-degree, spring-charged creek water, remains partially ice-free a few weeks longer. Once again, I have the silent aquifer to thank for an unexpected gift.

The body heat of the geese also helps to keep the water from freezing, and it's likely that trumpeter swans follow the calls of the geese to these areas of open water. When the lake finally freezes over completely in January, the swans can fly a few hundred yards up Pine Creek and pass the rest of the winter swimming among the concealing cattails and nutritious aquatic plants.

Finding the family of trumpeters at Pine Lake warms my heart and confirms in my mind that this prairie oasis remains mostly whole and healthy. I never considered my Sandhills hideaway pristine or completely natural, what with the paved road skirting the eastern lakeshore, the introduced red cedars invading lakeside meadows and adjacent dunes, and exotic pondweeds coating the lake surface in late summer. But this out-of-the-way state wildlife area always seems serene and full of life, and if the most magnificent water birds in North America have chosen it as their winter home, it might just measure up.

Around midmorning, as clouds of steam rise from the opening in the ice, all the geese take off with a flourish, leaving only the family of swans. They continue to cruise back and forth across the mirror-like surface for the rest of the day.

I take advantage of the warming sunlight and absence of wind to stroll to the north end of the lake, through the woods, and onto the snow-softened hills. Every once in a while I hear a faint "ko-honk" to the south, pause on a dune crest, and feel comforted by the sight of the glistening white swans and their handsome offspring creasing the placid water.

Sacred Gifts

On a glowing evening in early June, I sit on a smooth cottonwood log watching red admiral butterflies flit from one sunlit gooseberry leaf to another. Gentle ripples lap at my feet. In the dunes behind me, the pines creak and quiver in the dying breeze.

Just before sunset I wander south through the lakeside cottonwood grove, taking in the subdued late-day songs of wood-pewees, orioles, and doves. Tomorrow is the morning of my annual breeding bird survey, but on this peaceful evening, counting the birds or peering at them through binoculars is the farthest thing from my mind.

Nevertheless, a flash of white behind a low promontory on the near shore catches my eye and quickens my heartbeat. The apparition vanishes for a moment behind a clump of cattails. Then here come the two adult swans, easing around the promontory and gliding toward me.

I watch transfixed as they keep on coming, following the shoreline toward the quiet inlet below my campsite. It's only when they pass close by that I see two tiny cygnets bobbing up and down between them.

It almost feels like the adults have headed my way on purpose, wanting to show off their newly hatched young. And who could blame them? These furiously paddling balls of fluff are as precious as anything I've ever seen.

The trumpeter family settles into the inlet, where they spend the rest of the evening foraging, with the adults scattering bits of masticated pondweed across the surface and their cheeping offspring scurrying after the prized tidbits. From time to time the parents extend their graceful necks and gaze my way, but they hardly seem to notice me.

The following dawn, when I head out to count the birds, the swans are nowhere to be seen. Strolling south along the lakeshore, I encounter most of my familiar neighbors, including the male great crested flycatcher whooping warnings from his nest tree, yellow-headed blackbirds rasping and cawing from bending cattail stalks—even a wood duck, who shoots out of her nest cavity in a dying cottonwood as a woodland hawk glides by.

It's quieter up in the dunes, and I pause every few paces to photograph cerulean spiderwort blossoms, lemon-yellow wallflowers, and miniature, lime-green grasshoppers. From one of the highest dunes, I look back toward the lake and see the white-tailed doe standing in a grassy hollow fifty yards away.

Her brown eyes sparkle in the sunlight as she stares at me for a long minute before finally lowering her head to munch on some sand cherry leaves. Knowing that she must have a fawn lying out nearby, I avert my eyes and walk away slowly.

Back at camp, while enjoying a bowl of granola and a mug of coffee, I see the swans ease out of the cattail marsh at the north end of the lake. They spend the rest of the morning cruising across the inlet and feeding. The adults seem to synchronize the slow-motion immersion of their long necks into the water, gliding and dipping in unison, while the energetic young watch attentively for whatever might emerge from the depths.

When I sit quietly on a shaded log, the swans drift closer, until I can see water droplets plinking down from the adults' black bills and garlands of pondweed draped around their necks. The chicks zip around like windup toys, pecking at anything green they find on the surface.

Around noon a fishing skiff puts in from the small boat launch on the northeast side of the lake and putters toward the inlet. Silently and with no discernible effort, the swans glide to the north shore and dissolve into the cattails.

It's just a short stroll from the lakeshore up through the dunes to a peaceful napping spot beneath the tallest ponderosas. As I settle into the fragrant pine needles and begin to drift off, I envision a mossy knoll deep in the marsh where two downy cygnets nestle under their parents' fleecy white wings.

Fallen Star

The Plains Indian story about a young woman who marries a star, digs up a forbidden prairie turnip, and creates an illuminating porthole in the sky has many iterations. And it hardly ends with that one heart-wrenching scene.

Without radios, televisions, or printed books, peoples of the plains relied on story-telling around evening fires to communicate their traditions and knowledge. Some of these stories would go on for several nights, rambling from one episode to another. And they might change or branch out subtly as succeeding generations related them.

In one version of the story, the young woman becomes so overcome with grief and longing that she weaves together some vines to create a rope ladder and begins to descend from the clouds. But the ladder is not quite long enough, and she falls and is killed.

As it turns out, she is bearing a child, and that child survives the fall and is adopted by a family of wolves. Star Child becomes a friend to all the wild creatures, including Meadowlark and Magpie, who teach him to speak the peoples' language. He grows quickly and becomes a cultural hero, traveling from village to village to help people with their struggles.

At one village, he hears of a monstrous red bird who lives in the tallest mountain and abducts young girls. Seven girls have been taken. He journeys to the mountain and kills the giant bird, but he tells the people he is powerless to bring back the girls' bodies.

Instead, he places their spirits in the heavens to remind us to take good care of our children. You can still see the souls of the little girls today as seven bright stars, known to some as the Seven Sisters, or the Pleiades.

I'm touched by that image as well. At a time when our fractiousness and foolishness threaten the lives of our own schoolchildren, we still have the stars to instruct us. They tell me that the universe is full of infinite wonder and nurturing energy, and we need only watch, listen, and learn.

One evening last June, I stood on the lakeshore as the sunlight reflecting off a receding thundercloud set the prairie aglow. An astonishing triple rainbow arched across the water, where white pelicans bobbed up and down on frothy waves. Between the fiery lower arc and the lake surface, veils of glistening mist swirled up and melted away, revealing distant dunes basking in heavenly light.

As the storm rumbled eastward, the breeze softened and the lake surface rocked to a standstill. Standing in the last rays of the sinking sun, I felt the lake's humming resonance—the gathered murmurs of every living thing—pulse through me. I thought fondly of my mother and father; my loving wife, Nancy; devoted siblings, nieces, and nephews; a cradling web of cherished friends and wild companions. That moment felt like all anyone could ever wish for.

A Buddhist-inspired parable about life and death describes a broad river whose diverse elements flow together as one. The river comes to a high cliff and plunges down in a spectacular waterfall, shattering the current into millions of separate droplets. Each falling droplet represents a single life. At the bottom of the falls, the droplets flow back together and continue on their way.

From the instant of our birth, we feel this jarring separation, and as we go through life we yearn to reunite with family, community, and the life forces that have spawned and nourished us. We sense our abiding kinship with all living things when we gaze into the golden iris of a long-eared owl, feel the earthy breath of a white-tailed deer, or stand beneath an ethereal summer sky.

I've felt transformed by these moments, and I look forward to the next stage of the journey.

Acknowledgments

Seventy-five years ago, Sandhills homesteaders James M. Smith, Sue E. Smith, and Sadie M. Smith donated a spring-fed lake near the headwaters of Pine Creek to the people of Nebraska, "for their appreciation and enjoyment of wildlife." Over the next twenty years, Nebraska Game and Parks purchased additional acreage south and west of the lake. The donated lake and surrounding wetlands, woodlands, and grassy dunes now constitute one of the richest wildlife habitats on the western plains.

Nebraska Game and Parks maintains more than one hundred state wildlife management areas, all open to the public. While these areas were created primarily to support hunting and fishing, many offer rare opportunities for solitude and communion with nature. Several of these areas were partially donated by private landowners, and acquisition of others is funded by hunting licenses, fishing licenses, and user fees. Visitors can contribute to preservation of state wildlife areas by purchasing a Nebraska State Parks Pass and stipulating that an additional amount be donated to the state wildlife fund.

Dedicated wildlife staff accomplish exceptional things with limited funds. Nebraska Game and Parks waterfowl biologist Mark Vrtiska, who has overseen the recovery of trumpeter swans throughout the region, provided invaluable information about the swans' behavior and ecological needs. Northwest Nebraska regional wildlife manager Hunter Baillie and his field staff helped me understand the origins of protected lands within the Pine Creek drainage.

Crescent Lake National Wildlife Refuge wildlife biologist Marlin French answered innumerable questions and apprised me of ongoing changes in the landscape. He and other federal government employees work heroically to maintain the largest protected areas within the Sandhills, including Crescent Lake, Valentine, and Fort Niobrara national wildlife refuges; Nebraska National Forest; and two wilderness areas. Their work ensures that this region continues to provide viable habitat for most naturally occurring species. Hundreds of thousands of acres of land protected by the Nature Conservancy, other conservation organizations, private landowners, and the University of Nebraska contribute to this effort.

Sandhills ranchers work from dawn to dusk to make sure the grasslands remain healthy and productive. I'm thankful to the dozens of residents who stopped to talk with me along back roads or invited me into their homes. I'm particularly grateful to Cynthia Miller, Dennis Miller, and Jean Jensen of The Most Unlikely Place Art Gallery and Café in Lewellen and to Bruce Burdick of the Lewellen visitors committee for welcoming ecotourists while protecting habitat for migrating cranes.

Several friends and colleagues reviewed much or all of the manuscript and offered very useful suggestions. My heartfelt thanks go out to Merrill Gilfillan, Chris Hoffman, Kristen Marshall, Christina Nealson, Anne-Marie Odasz, and John O'Keefe.

Geoffrey Ames accompanied me on a half dozen sublime camping trips to the western plains, sharing numerous insights concerning the interplay of landscape, history, and culture. Others who joined me in the Sandhills include Zoe Ames, Linda Bevard, Scott Brown, George Durazzo and Sandra Halin-Adams, Patrick Jones, Peter Jones, Elena Klaver, Joe and Pam Piombino, Mary Stuber, Roger Verley, John Weller, and the Boulder County Audubon teen naturalists and their parents. Thank you for your quiet enthusiasm and your tolerance of a naturalist's single-minded obsessions.

Nancy Dawson, my loving partner of forty years, repeatedly encouraged me to go off on my own and find whatever I might be looking for, then reviewed the entire manuscript, improving it immensely. My friend and colleague Chris Hoffman encouraged me all the way through and critiqued an early draft, launching the book on its crooked path toward coherence.

Executive editor Clark Whitehorn and the editorial staff at University of Nebraska Press showed faith in the book from the beginning and escorted it seamlessly through editing and production. I'm particularly thankful to Amanda Jackson for her sensitive and insightful editing, publicity manager Rosemary Sekora for her enthusiasm and creative support, and senior project editor Sara Springsteen for keeping us all on the same page.

The primary contributors to this book are my treasured companions at the lake. There's the family of long-eared owls who converse with me at night while defending their nest from invasive crows and great horned owls; the white-tailed doe who confronts me on June mornings and guides me away from her helpless fawn; the pair of trumpeter swans who escort their newly hatched young across the water, only to see most of them plucked from the surface by introduced predators.

Their courage and grace illuminate this story, and in the end, this book is for them. May they persevere, prosper, and continue to teach us how to live.

Notes

Portal in the Sky

This version of the traditional story about a young woman who marries a star and creates a revelatory hole in the sky when she pulls up a giant prairie turnip follows the George Bird Grinnell late-nineteenth-century translation reprinted in *By Cheyenne Campfires* (Lincoln: University of Nebraska Press, 1971). The Lakota-maintained Oceti Sakowin Essential Understandings website, www.wolakotaproject.org, includes a wealth of information about Native uses of the prairie turnip, along with a video showing Duane Hollow Horn Bear's telling of the story.

The rendition in this chapter is only the first part; "Fallen Star," in this volume, includes a short summary of one version of its continuation.

Timpsula

Sandhills thunderstorms are among the most violent and scary on earth. Some areas of the western plains receive as many as one hundred thunderstorms per year. Recent studies suggest that thunderstorms are likely to grow more frequent and more severe as global warming progresses. See Robert J. Trapp et al., "Changes in Severe Thunderstorm Environmental Frequency in the 21st Century Caused by Anthropogenically Induced Climate Change," *Proceedings of the National Academy of Science* 104, no. 50 (1971): 9–23.

Kelly Kindscher's book *Edible Wild Plants of the Prairie* (Lawrence: University Press of Kansas, 1992) describes both subsistence and ceremonial uses of prairie turnips, known to Lakota peoples as *tipsinna* or *timpsula*. John Farrar includes a photo and detailed description in his *Wildflowers of Nebraska and the Great Plains* (Lincoln: Nebraska Game and Parks Commission, 1990).

Owls

The "Drying Grass Moon" (Lakota term), known to many European Americans as the harvest moon, rises within an hour of sunset for five consecutive days, due to interaction between Earth's tilt and the lunar orbit. In other words, the moonrise retards only about thirty minutes per evening in September, whereas the amount is close to ninety minutes per evening in March. This apparent anomaly is created by the angle of the moonrise relative to the horizon. Having the full moon rise so close to sunset night after night gives farmers more light by which to harvest their crops, hence the European name "harvest moon."

The decline in long-eared owl populations throughout areas of western North America seems to stem from fragmentation of riparian and grassland ecosystems by humans, which has enabled urban-adapted predators, including great horned owls and American crows, to prey upon long-eared owl nests. See J. S. Marks, D. L. Evans, and D. W. Holt, "Long-eared Owl (*Asio otus*)," in *The Birds of North America* online, www.allaboutbirds.org, edited by A. F. Poole and F. B. Gill (Ithaca: Cornell Lab of Ornithology, 1994).

Feather's Touch

Chris Hoffman's book *The Hoop and the Tree* (Chicago Review Press, 2021) reveals how cultures around the world have used hoop and tree symbolism to describe our roots, strivings, and relationships. The book also provides myriad examples of how we can use this knowledge to enrich our lives and our relationships with the natural world.

Crescent Lake National Wildlife Refuge is one of three national wildlife refuges within the Sandhills region. Encompassing nearly 150,000 acres, the refuges are managed to conserve and restore habitat for native wildlife. The federal government has been reducing staffing at these refuges for years, and there has even been discussion of selling off Crescent Lake National Wildlife Refuge, a virtual paradise for breeding birds and naturalists, to private interests.

The bird I refer to as juniper solitaire is still described by the American Ornithological Society as "Townsend's solitaire." John Kirk Townsend was an American physician who collected a number of bird and mammal species during the first half of the nineteenth century. Throughout this book I've tried to show respect for other beings by not using possessive names of people, mostly European and North American males who "collected" them or purchased their stuffed carcasses from other collectors, to describe them. A growing movement within North America has petitioned the American Ornithological Society to change all the patronymic names currently being used to describe 149 North American bird species. For more information, visit the Bird Names for Birds website, https://birdnamesforbirds.wordpress.com.

The fall sandhill crane migration through Nebraska usually peaks in early October. More than a half million cranes fly through on their way south from nesting areas extending from the central Rockies and Great Lakes region to Alaska and Siberia. In March and early April, more than five hundred thousand lesser sandhill cranes pause for a month or so along the central Platte and North Platte Rivers to rest and refuel before continuing north. Visit the Lillian Annette Rowe Audubon Sanctuary website, https://rowe.audubon.org/, for viewing information.

Ojo de Agua

An Atlas of the Sand Hills, edited by Ann Bleed and Charles Flowerday (Lincoln: Conservation and Survey Division, University of Nebraska, 1989) provides comprehensive information about the High Plains aquifer, including flows and rates of depletion.

For a more recent in-depth account of the decline and uncertain future of the High Plains aquifer, see Jeremy Frankel, "Crisis on the High Plains: The Loss of North America's Largest Aquifer— the Ogallala," *University of Denver Water Law Review*, May 17, 2018, http://duwaterlawreview.com/crisis-on-the-high-plains-the-loss-of-americas-largest-aquifer-the-ogallala/.

Denise Sammons writes about the magic of Sandhills artesian springs on the National Water Center website, www.nationalwatercentervintage.org.

Ward Rutherford describes Irish traditional beliefs concerning naturally occurring springs in *Celtic Mythology* (San Francisco: Weiser Books, 2015).

For a more complete version of the story about the old woman at the spring, see George Dorsey, *Pawnee Mythology* (Lincoln: University of Nebraska Press, 1997).

Don Kroodsma provides fascinating observations of song-dueling among marsh wrens in the *Singing Life of Birds* (New York: Houghton-Mifflin, 2005).

In January 2021 the Biden administration withdrew the federal permit for construction of the Keystone Pipeline, but that doesn't guarantee that the pipeline will go away forever. Lawsuits and petitions to state and federal government will likely continue for years, and completed sections of the pipeline may continue to pump oil. See Mose Buchele, "The Keystone XL Pipeline Is Dead Again. What Does That Mean for Texas?" KUT 90.5 National Public Radio Austin, January 25, 2021, www.kut.org.

John Marsden's *Where the Sky Began: Land of the Tallgrass Prairie* (Ames: University of Iowa Press, 1995) celebrates the beauty and ecology of one of our most endangered ecosystems.

Dawn Chorus

Thirussawichi's description of the dawn was quoted by George Bird Grinnell in *Pawnee, Blackfoot, and Cheyenne: History and Folklore of the Plains* (New York: Scribner, 1961).

I substituted a more respectful common name for the woodland hawk, still referred to as "Cooper's hawk" by the American Ornithological Society.

The North American Breeding Bird Survey is a cooperative project of the U.S. Geological Service Patuxent Wildlife Research Center and the Canadian government. Volunteers drive more than five hundred survey routes throughout North America once each year, counting birds from each of fifty point-count stations. Because the surveys are conducted by volunteers (and possibly because survey data are used to support enforcement of long-standing federal acts that protect nesting bird populations), the Trump administration restricted public access to data from these surveys. For the most recent available data, visit www.pwrc.usgs.gov/bbs.

Corn ethanol does produce slightly more energy than is required to plant, process, and convert the corn, but other second-generation biofuels, including switchgrass, do better. See the U.S. Department of Energy's Alternative Fuels Data Center website, https://afdc.energy.gov, to access a number of recent studies.

The Illinois College of Agriculture, Consumer and Environmental Resources study of impacts of declining insect numbers on bird populations was summarized in "Decline in U.S. Bird Biodiversity Related to Neonicotinoids, Study Shows," *Science Daily*, August 14, 2020, www.sciencedaily.com. The study concluded that grassland bird numbers had declined nationwide by 53 percent since 1970.

For information about a variety of comprehensive studies of the relationship of grazing, fire, and other activities to grassland structure and grassland bird populations, visit the Konza Prairie Biological Station website, https://kpbs.konza.k-state.edu.

Results of the study showing almost universal failure of mallard nests in an eastern Sandhills study area are reported in J. Walker, L. Powell, Z. Cunningham, M. Vrtiska, and S. Stephens, "Low Reproductive Success of Mallards in a Grassland Dominated Landscape in the Sandhills of Nebraska," *Prairie Naturalist* 40, no. 1/2 (May/June 2008).

Insect die-offs that have occurred throughout the world, while often caused by use of toxic chemicals, are also being driven by climate change. A summary of butterfly surveys carried out in the western United States during the past four decades concluded that butterfly numbers throughout the region have declined by as much as 25 percent, with drying vegetation and proliferation of fires driving the decline. See Dino Grandoni, "Butterflies Are Vanishing Out West. Scientists Say Climate Change Is to Blame," *Washington Post*, March 4, 2021.

A 2018 U.S. Fish and Wildlife Service report estimated that an average of 2.4 billion birds are killed each year in the United States by cats and six hundred million by collisions with building glass. See "Threats to Birds," U.S. Fish and Wildlife Service, September 14, 2018, www.fws.gov/birds.

Shorebirds in the Grass

To learn more about red crossbill behavior and species differentiation, visit the red crossbill species account by C. W. Benkman and M. A. Young, in *The Birds of North America* online, www .allaboutbirds.org (2019).

William Henry Hudson describes the solitary flight of migrating upland sandpipers in *A Hind in Richmond Park: The Collected Works of William Henry Hudson* (Houston: Hardpress, 2014).

For a review of long-billed curlew nesting behavior, ecology, and population trends, see R. D. Dugger and K. E. Dugger, "Long-Billed Curlew," in *The Birds of North America* online, www.allaboutbirds .org (2002). Curlew population trend information is available at the Patuxent Wildlife Center North American Breeding Bird Survey site. Also see Julia Allen's fascinating monograph "The Ecology and Behavior of the Long-Billed Curlew in Southeastern Washington," *Wildlife Monographs*, no.73 (October 1980).

National Audubon Society naturalist Amy Lewis chronicles the decline of curlews throughout the world in "The Eskimo Curlew Hasn't Been Seen in 55 Years. Is It Time to Declare It Extinct?" April 20, 2018, www.audubon.org.

For a compilation of quotes about curlews, including several from Robert Burns, visit the Caught by the River website, www .caughtbytheriver.net.

Swan Lake

The Trumpeter Swan Society, headquartered in Plymouth, Minnesota, has advocated successfully for conservation of trumpeter swan nesting habitat and populations for more than eighty years. Their website, www.trumpeterswansociety.org, includes a wealth of information about populations, nesting behaviors, ongoing studies, and conservation challenges.

Stephanie Johnson and Mark Vrtiska, with Nebraska Game and Parks, have been carrying out a comprehensive study of trumpeter swan nesting success throughout the Sandhills. They report some of their initial findings and give a history of trumpeter swans in Nebraska on the Birds of Nebraska website, https:// birds.outdoornebraska.gov.

Black Cherry Moon

For a thorough description of the Lakota sun dance ritual, see Joseph E. Brown, *The Sacred Pipe: Black Elk's Account of the Seven Rights of the Oglala Sioux* (Norman: University of Oklahoma Press, 1989).

For a summary of research on how grasses use chemicals to lure wasps that prey on grass-consuming caterpillars, see "Mown Grass Smell Sends sos for Help in Resisting Insect Attacks," *Agrilife Today*, September 14, 2014.

Robin Kimmerer describes the wonders and traditional uses of sweetgrass in the preface of *Braiding Sweetgrass: Indigenous Wisdom, Scientific Knowledge, and the Teaching of Plants* (Minneapolis MN: Milkweed Editions, 2013).

Milkweed Silk

For a detailed discussion of the various uses of milkweed, including descriptions of Native American uses, see Kelly Kindscher, *Edible Wild Plants of the Prairie* (Lawrence: University Press of Kansas, 1992).

Anurag Agrawal's fascinating book *Monarchs and Milkweed* (Princeton NJ: Princeton University Press, 2017) offers intimate descriptions of scientific research on milkweed blossoms, milkweed distribution, and the competitive and sometimes deadly interactions between monarch caterpillars and milkweed plants.

The Ogallala Down Company continues to make mattresses stuffed with milkweed silk. Visit their website, www.ogallalacomfort.com.

For a user-friendly introductory field guide to milkweed insects, see *Milkweed, Monarchs, and More*, by Ba Rea and Karen Overhauser (Bas Relief Publishing Group, 2010).

Snow Blows like Spirits in the Sun

Ora A. Clement writes about the "Schoolchildren's Storm" in *Roundup: A Nebraska Reader*, edited by Virginia Faulkner (Lincoln: University of Nebraska Press, 1957).

The "Starvation Winter of the Blackfeet" is described by Helen B. West in *Montana: The Magazine of Western History* 9 (Winter 1959): 4–16.

Bernd Heinrich writes in fascinating detail about winter survival strategies of birds and amphibians in *Winter World* (New York: HarperCollins, 2003).

Popping Trees

Plains Indian names for various moons can vary from place to place and year to year, depending on circumstances and weather. The first moon of winter has been referred to by the Lakotas as "Moon of Shedding Antlers" and "Moon of Popping Trees." Lakota journalist Tim Giago uses the latter term in his account of the Wounded Knee Massacre. Giago, the first Native American to receive the South Dakota distinguished journalist award, published his description of the Wounded Knee Massacre in "The Moon of the Popping Trees," in the December 31, 2012, and February 14, 2014, editions of the *Huffington Post*, www.huffpost.com.

Rex Smith uses the term in his 1975 book *Moon of Popping Trees* (Lincoln: University of Nebraska Press, 1975), the most detailed published description of events leading up to the Wounded Knee Massacre. Smith's treatment does include some speculation about what various participants, especially Native Americans, were thinking at various times. Another European American writer, Dee Brown, gives a concise summary of the events from a mostly Native American perspective in *Bury My Heart at Wounded Knee* (New York: Sterling Signature, 1970 and 2000).

Spotted Tail described the Lakota reasons for declining the settlement recommended by the Supreme Court on the August 24, 2011, broadcast of *PBS News Hour*, www.pbs.org/newshour.

Daniel Wildcat explained why reparations can't compensate for loss of land in a June 11, 2014, post "Why Native Americans Don't Want Reparations," *Post Everything*, www.washingtonpost.com/posteverything.

Anna V. Smith summarizes the decades-old debate over Oregon Native lands reparations in "Federal Lands Are Becoming Tribal Lands Again," *Mother Jones*, August 17, 2019.

The quote from Luther Standing Bear is included in his book *My Indian Boyhood* (Lincoln NE: Bison Books, 2006).

For more information about the composition of the Sioux Nation, see "Understanding the Great Sioux Nation," at the Akta Lakota Museum and Cultural Center website, http://aktalakota.stjo.org.

The Encyclopedia of the Great Plains, edited by David J. Wishart, offers a summary of Sioux culture and history, as well as the tragic history of the Pawnees and Poncas: http://plainshumanities .unl.edu/encyclopedia/doc/egp.na.107.

Turtle Tears

For details about ornate box turtle habitat and movement patterns in the Sandhills, see A. J. Redder, C. K. Todd, D. McDonald, and D. A. Keinath, "Ornate Box Turtle (*Terrapene ornata ornata*), a Technical Conservation Assessment," U.S. Department of Agriculture Forest Service, 2006.

Phillipe de Vosjoli and Roger Klingenberg summarize various reports of box turtle longevity in *The Box Turtle Manual* (Advanced Vivarium Systems, 2004).

Robin Wall Kimmerer provides breathtaking renditions of Turtle Island creation stories in *Braiding Sweetgrass: Indigenous Wisdom, Scientific Knowledge, and the Teachings of Plants* (Minneapolis MN: Milkweed Editions, 2013).

Construction of wildlife underpasses to conserve Blanding's turtle populations in the eastern Sandhills is profiled in Blake Ursch's "Blanding's Turtle, Endangered in Many Areas, Has Found a Happy Home in the Nebraska Sandhills," *Omaha World Herald*, August 1, 2017.

Circles of Life

As of December 2019, the American Bird Conservancy estimated the total North American wild turkey population at 7.8 million. Their website, https://abcbirds.org, includes an engaging summary of turkey behavior and conservation challenges.

Recovery of river otters throughout Nebraska is described by Nebraska Game and Parks biologist Sarah Nevison in "River Otters, an Unprecedented Conservation Success Story," in the 2020 newsletter from the Nebraska Wildlife Conservation Fund.

Piping plovers are listed as threatened by Nebraska Game and Parks, who include striking photos of piping plover nests and nesting habitat on the Birds of Nebraska website, https://birds.outdoornebraska.gov.

For a photo and good description of blowout penstemon, see John Farrar, *Wildflowers of Nebraska and the Great Plains* (Lincoln: Nebraska Game and Parks Commission, 1990).

A study of burrowing owls in South Dakota concluded that a significant landscape factor that precludes nesting is the presence of trees within proximity of potential nest burrows. J. P. Thiele, K. K. Bakker, and C. D. Dieter, "Multiscale Nest Site Selection by Burrowing Owls in South Dakota," *Wilson Bulletin* 125, no. 4 (December 2013): 763–74.

The Rights of Nature: A Legal Revolution That Could Save the World, by David Boyd (Toronto: ECW Press, 2017), profiles the history of the rights of nature movement and describes successful application of the principle by indigenous peoples and urban communities.

In *The Hoop and the Tree, a Compass for Finding a Deeper Relationship with All Life* (Chicago: Chicago Review Press, 2021), Chris Hoffman describes how cultures throughout the world have used hoop imagery to represent family, community, and our relationship with nature and tree imagery to represent striving, growth, and reaching toward the divine. "When you begin to embody the Hoop and the Tree you grow rooted and fruitful, humble and whole," he writes. "You put yourself at home in the universe, in the flow of life, nurturing, sustaining, and honoring the Great Mystery, and supported by it."

Black Elk describes his great vision in *Black Elk Speaks: Being the Life Story of a Holy Man of the Oglala Sioux*, as told through John G. Neihardt (Lincoln: University of Nebraska Press, 1988), 43.

Path of Souls

Hear snowy tree cricket cadences at various temperatures and read about their life history on the University of Florida Department of Entomology website, https://entnemdept.ufl.edu.

Laboratory studies show that female crickets are attracted by the rapidity of the males' chirping, rather than by warmer male body temperatures. See Bettina Erreger, R. Mathias Henning, and

Heiner Romer, "The 'Hot Male' Hypothesis: Do Females Prefer Males with Increased Body Temperature in Mate Choice Scenarios?" *Animal Behavior* 138 (April 2018): 75–84.

Nathaniel Hawthorne's descriptions of crickets were included in an 1846 collection of short stories titled *Mosses from an Old Manse* (New York: Modern Library Classics, 2003).

For more information about conservation threats to northern harriers, see K. G. Smith, S. R. Wittenberg, R. B. MacWhirtier, and K. L. Bildstein, "Northern Harrier," in *The Birds of North America* online, www.allaboutbirds.org (2011).

Short-eared owl conservation and population trends in Colorado are reviewed in Lynn Wickersham, ed., *The Second Colorado Breeding Bird Atlas* (Denver: Colorado Bird Atlas Partnership, 2016); they are reviewed in Nebraska by Wayne J. Molhoff, "The Second Nebraska Breeding Bird Atlas," *Bulletin of the University of Nebraska State Museum* 29 (2016).

Edwin Barnhart describes Native American beliefs concerning the Path of Souls in "The Milky Way as the Path to the Otherworld: A Comparison of Pre-Columbian New-World Cultures," Maya Exploration Center, September 2003, www.mayaexploration .org. William B. Powers also explores these beliefs in *Oglala Religion* (Lincoln: University of Nebraska Press, 1977).

Grace

Despite liberalized hunting seasons, the North American snow goose population has continued to rise to more than fifteen million. After hunting and habitat loss decimated their populations during the nineteenth and early twentieth centuries, breeding colonies became confined to isolated areas on the arctic plain.

Populations began to rebound during the late twentieth century as hunting was regulated and wintering geese learned to forage successfully in agricultural fields. Nesting snow geese, who are strongly attached to historic nesting colonies, began to overpopulate and denude the tundra in these sites, leading to starvation of adults and young, along with the loss of vast areas of native vegetation.

This does not necessarily mean that there are "too many snow geese," as people often assert. (There are actually twenty-five times as many humans as snow geese in North America, and we are much more destructive.) It means that, once again, our actions have created imbalance and stress in the natural world, with tragic results. See "Lifting Hunting Limits Hasn't Solved the Snow Goose Overpopulation Problem," *American Ornithological Society*, May 23, 2019; and "Snow Goose Boom Could Lead to Ecological Disaster," *Springfield News Leader*, March 2, 2018.

Sacred Gifts

Sadly, both cygnets vanished during the summer months, likely victims of predation by snapping turtles or predatory fish. While keeping track of swan families, it's heartbreaking to see recently hatched young disappear year after year and, in the fall, to watch adults cruise across their home lakes with no young to accompany them. One summer at Arthur County Swan Lake I counted fifteen cygnets swimming with three adult pairs in early June and only three remaining cygnets in late September.

Still, the Sandhills population keeps increasing gradually, thanks to the adults' ten years or more of breeding productivity and to the protection of existing nest sites from human disturbance.

Fallen Star

This version of the "Fallen Star and Star Boy" story is recounted by Lakota elder Duane Hollow Horn Bear on the Oceti Sakowin Essential Understandings website, www.wolakotaproject.org.